NOTHING SO ABSURD

NOTHING SO ABSURD

An Invitation to Philosophy

PHILLIP HOFFMANN

broadview press

National Library of Canada Cataloguing in Publication

Hoffmann, Phillip, 1956 –
    Nothing so absurd : an invitation to philosophy / Phillip Hoffmann.

Includes bibliographical references and index.
ISBN 1-55111-408-9

1. Philosophy—Introductions. I. Title.

BD21.H64 2003   100   C2003-904195-6

Broadview Press Ltd. is an independent, international publishing house, incorporated in 1985. Broadview believes in shared ownership, both with its employees and with the general public; since the year 2000 Broadview shares have traded publicly on the Toronto Venture Exchange under the symbol BDP.

We welcome comments and suggestions regarding any aspect of our publications–please feel free to contact us at the addresses below or at broadview@broadviewpress.com.

North America
PO Box 1243, Peterborough, Ontario, Canada K9J 7H5
Tel: (705) 743-8990; Fax: (705) 743-8353
email: customerservice@broadviewpress.com
3576 California Road, Orchard Park, NY, USA 14127

UK, Ireland, and continental Europe
Plymbridge Distributors Ltd.
Estover Road,
Plymouth, PL6 7PY, UK
Tel: (01752) 202301; Fax: (01752) 202333
email: orders@plymbridge.com

Australia and New Zealand
UNIREPS, University of New South Wales
Sydney, NSW, 2052
Tel: 61 2 9664 0999; Fax: 61 2 9664 5420
email: info.press@unsw.edu.au
www.broadviewpress.com

Eco-Logo Certified
30 % Post.

To Ingrid, in fulfillment of a promise made long ago, and to the memory of Albert Polsky (1925–2001).

Contents

Acknowledgements

I have accrued debts to a number of individuals and organizations in the course of writing this book. Foremost among these are the Philosophy Department and Faculty of Continuing Education at the University of Calgary for having given me abundant opportunities to learn and teach philosophy. In particular, I wish to thank Professors C.B. Martin, John Heintz, Jack MacIntosh, and David Sharp (University of Alberta) for years of counsel, scholarly assistance and encouragement. Without the support and confidence of Janet Sisson and Don LePan, I might never have completed this project. Thanks to DeVry Institute of Technology, Calgary, for a sabbatical in the summer of 2000, during which I completed two chapters of the book. Colleagues and students of mine at DeVry have enriched and furthered my teaching career in ways too numerous to detail. I owe special thanks to Maria Neuwirth, Graham Bolton, Allan Brown, and Stephanie Davis for reading various draft chapters and excerpts, and for providing me with valuable feedback and insights. Like all teachers, I learn from my students, and am grateful to them for what they have taught me about pedagogy and philosophy. I especially want to thank Louise Feroze, Jacquie Jacobi, Peter Pavey, Andre Lanz and Brendan O'Connor for the friendships that grew out of their participation in one of my courses. I owe the idea of the multiple meanings of life in § 6.7 to discussions with Ivan Zendel. Special thanks go to

Jude Polsky for her love, support, guidance, generosity, and superb editorial assistance. The duck-rabbit image in Figure 1 comes courtesy of <www.alphalink.com.au/~park/images/image8.htm>. Finally, I want to thank three anonymous reviewers for Broadview Press and John Burbidge, whose valuable criticisms of earlier drafts made for a better book than I could otherwise have written. Whatever shortcomings remain redound to me alone.

Preface

This book grew out of lectures I presented in an introductory philosophy course that I taught for many years through the Faculty of Continuing Education at the University of Calgary. The main challenge I faced in those lectures was to find ways to make philosophy—more specifically topics in Western philosophy—lively and relevant to course participants with diverse backgrounds, educations and ages, but who were all motivated to learn more about the subject.

The challenge had a number of aspects. First, I needed to identify and discuss preconceptions about the nature of philosophy itself. In addition, I had to find ways to pitch the subject at a level neither too simplistic nor too advanced for a general audience. I wanted to strike a balance between presenting an historical overview of Western philosophy and outlining the views of specific philosophers on particular topics. Like all teachers of philosophy, I had to be prepared to defend positions to the inevitable question: "Yes, but what are *your* views on this issue?" Finally, I had to be alert to the kinds of interests, concerns and questions that participants were likely to have about the material under discussion. I do not advance detailed, original arguments on every topic in every chapter, but the book you are holding comprises my best effort to explain and understand those topics myself.

This book is aimed at students and general readers who have

an interest in philosophy, but who might not want to indulge this interest beyond the level of a non-credit or a first credit course in the subject. On the other hand, I would be delighted if reading this book inspires you to delve into philosophy further than that. To this end, I have included a brief annotated list of further readings and electronic resources at the end of the book. Of those works, two in particular deserve special recognition. I used Robert Solomon's *Introducing Philosophy* for many years and recommend it as a highly effective textbook for teaching non-credit, introductory philosophy courses; and I drew upon Rudy Rucker's thoughts about Richard's Paradox in *Infinity and the Mind* for the main argument in § 3.6.

Acting on the advice that book sales would be halved for every equation he included, Stephen Hawking steered clear of all but one equation in his hugely successful book *A Brief History of Time*. Since this is a philosophy book rather than one about physics, I didn't have to worry about equations, but I have tried hard to keep philosophical jargon at a minimum, especially "isms." Like Hawking, I learned that presenting abstract and difficult ideas to a general audience without sacrificing rigour is very tricky, but I found avoiding all "isms" was impractical. With the exception of some passing references to determinism, Darwinism, monism and pluralism, I restricted myself to discussing only four "isms" in any detail: *metaphysical realism*, *relativism*, *skepticism*, and *solipsism*. Hawking used just one equation in his book, but if as a result I reach an audience only a quarter the size of Hawking's, I will be more than satisfied.

What is Philosophy?

There is nothing so absurd that some philosopher has not said it.

— CICERO

WHAT PHILOSOPHY IS NOT

Defining the nature of philosophy is no easy task, but in order to understand philosophy, we should first say something about what it is not and perhaps dispel a few myths at the same time. The idea of explaining something indirectly, in terms of what it is not rather than what it is, is itself a philosophical technique that dates back to antiquity, and is known as the *via negativa*.

Philosophy is neither a religion nor a science nor a self-help movement, although it does share elements with all of these pursuits. Philosophy, like religion, takes on questions about the meaning and purpose of our lives, our accountability for our thoughts and deeds, and the origins and fate of life and the universe. But unlike religion, philosophy does not rely on dogmas, doctrines or scriptures, nor does it provide definitive answers to such questions. Philosophers will often take a stand on an issue, but in general philosophy is not about being dogmatic, nor is it about uncritically accepting just any claim or claims. Nor, for that matter, is it about raising doubts simply for the sake of raising doubts. Like science, philosophy aims to understand the inner workings of nature, to find out whether the world is subject to laws of any kind, and it seeks to learn about our minds and how they operate. But philosophers do not perform experiments, do not work in laboratories and do not formulate their theories in accordance with the strict and specific methods of science. Like personal growth movements, philosophy tackles questions about our potential as humans, who we are and how we should conduct ourselves. However, philosophy encompasses much more than this, and in any case tends to have little to do with fads such as psychic channeling, claims about the power of crystals, and other New Age trappings.

How Philosophy Differs From Other Subjects

What kinds of things exist? Is the world made up of many things, or is there ultimately only one thing? Is there a God? What can we justifiably claim to know? Are any of our values objective, or are they all relative and subjective? What is the relationship between the mind and the body? These are some of the issues that comprise philosophy. To the extent that philosophy deals with such questions, it is different from other academic subjects in a variety of ways.

Most subjects begin with some basic concepts and ideas and build upon them to enable students to master more advanced material. Students learning mathematics, for example, typically begin with arithmetic before taking courses in calculus, non-linear algebra, or other more advanced areas of math. But in this respect, philosophy is very different. There are no easy, introductory steps when it comes to doing philosophy. As soon as we start posing philosophical questions, we immediately confront some of the deepest and most profound questions ever formulated. This aspect of philosophy can be bewildering, humbling, and daunting for beginners and experts alike, but on the other hand it is also exhilarating to realize that many of the problems we are investigating have troubled some of the greatest minds in history. To search for answers to philosophical problems is to embark upon a vast, ongoing, intellectual adventure along with the rest of humankind. In terms of a familiar metaphor, if philosophy were a swimming pool, it would have no shallow end; we are all in at the deep end. And while no instructor of an introductory math course would assign students unsolved math problems that have stumped mathematicians for centuries, the beginning philosopher is in precisely this predicament.

Secondly, philosophy is in a sense about itself, which is reminiscent of Jerry Seinfeld's description of the sitcom *Seinfeld* as being a show about itself. For example, the question *What is philosophy?* is itself a philosophical question. This contrasts with other disciplines such as economics, chemistry and anthropology. While there is no shortage of debates and competing theories within economics, for example, such as the debate between monetarists and supply-side economists, the question *What is economics?* is not a question *of* economics. It is, rather, a philosophical question. In fact, as soon as we even begin to reflect on what philosophy is, we begin to philosophize. The phenomenon of self-reference, which pops up again and again in philosophy, turns out to be a strange but extremely significant one. As we shall see later, it is responsible for not only some of the most exciting results, but also some of the deepest puzzles in contemporary philosophy.

As a general rule, the more one studies a subject at the post-secondary level, be it in the sciences or humanities, the more specialized one's study becomes. Studying literature at the graduate level, for example, might lead one to specialize in, say, modern Canadian literature or early medieval English literature. While philosophy can certainly be highly specialized and technical as well, it is a little different in this regard in that it also remains the broadest and most general of disciplines. As we noted above, inquiries into the nature of economics or anthropology or science are essentially inquiries of a philosophical nature. Philosophers are generalists at heart who, while not necessarily laying claim to having expert knowledge of any particular subject in the arts or sciences, cannot afford to ignore those subjects either, or at least not their foundations. For example, no philosopher with a serious interest in the nature of the mind can disregard important findings in psychology; a philosopher specializing in science obviously needs to be well informed about science; and so on.

While not everyone is a brain surgeon or an opera singer, virtually all of us practice philosophy, at least to some extent and at various points in our lives. Whenever we formulate fundamental beliefs and convictions about ourselves, beliefs that dictate our basic outlooks on life and through which we define ourselves, we are philosophers. But exactly what kinds of fundamental beliefs and convictions are we talking about, and how do they define us? These questions are difficult to answer, but the search for answers lies at the heart of this book.

THE WORD "PHILOSOPHY"

We are now in a position to start discussing the nature of philosophy in a positive sense. Let us begin with the word "philosophy" itself.

"Philosophy" comes from the ancient Greek word *philosophia*, which means "love of wisdom." The two roots of the original Greek word still survive in other modern-day English words such as "anglo*phile*" and "*soph*isticated." This is a useful start, but it brings in its wake further questions, such as What is wisdom? Wisdom is a somewhat nebulous concept, and it does not necessarily reside in having any specific piece of knowledge. Rather, it refers to the possession of deep insights or understanding, as well, perhaps, as the capacity to exercise good judgment on the basis of these insights. More specifically, a wise person is someone who has keen insights about the human condition. This picture of philosophy—philosophy-as-wisdom—where wisdom is construed as insight of a certain kind, is articulated by Socrates (469–399 B.C.E.) in his famous entreaty: know thyself. On this conception, philosophy becomes essentially a kind of process or activity, one that may vary in nature from person to person, both in terms of the practice of philosophy and in terms of what it might mean for different individuals.

What about the word "philosophy" itself? As we have noted, the word originated in ancient Greece. At the center of the ancient Greek world was the city-state of Athens, which flourished only for a relatively brief period around the fifth century B.C.E. To some extent, philosophy is an intellectual artifact of ancient Greek culture, one which lives on today in the West because we are the inheritors of that cultural tradition. Certainly it is difficult to underestimate the influence of the Greek philosophers on the history of ideas in the West. A.N. Whitehead (1861–1947), for instance, once remarked that Western philosophy is essentially a series of footnotes to Plato (427–347 B.C.E.). Whitehead's tribute to Plato's brilliance and the extent to which our own philosophical concerns have been shaped by issues which preoccupied Plato may be overstated, but his point is well taken. The German philosopher Martin Heidegger (1889–1976) also argued that the very notion of philosophy is thoroughly Greek in nature. If this is right, it would follow that, strictly speaking, it is problematic even to speak of, say, "Indian philosophy" or "Chinese philosophy." So what can we conclude about the universality of the notion of philosophy?

On the one hand virtually all cultures have furnished accounts of the general nature of the world, its origins, and our place in it, most usually in religious or mythological terms. Construed in this broad sense, philosophy is by no means confined to Western thought. But contemporary Western philosophy, with its emphasis on the careful analysis of language, meaning, reason, and logic—all of which were hallmarks of ancient Greek philosophy—is indeed the progeny of Greek thought. Further complicating matters is the problem of translation between languages, which the philosopher W.V. Quine (1908–2000) has done much to expose. According to Quine, we cannot know for certain how closely the original Greek word "φιλοσοφία" correlates with our own word "philosophy." After all, ancient Greek and modern English are two quite different languages. And by the same token, we cannot be confident that translations and transliterations of the word "philosophy" into languages such as Hindi, Arabic, Swahili, Mandarin, Estonian, and so on, are particularly precise.

What is the significance of these problems of universality and translation? There are no easy answers, but I would venture to say that there are enough commonalities between the people of world to qualify reference to "Indian philosophy" or "Chinese philosophy" as legitimate, notwithstanding Quine's argument and the many cultural and linguistic differences that clearly exist between India, China, and the West. To be sure, translation is a tricky undertaking, and no one would deny that Western civilization is highly indebted to the ancient Greeks. The concerns Heidegger and Quine raised cannot be dismissed lightly, but I shall leave them with you. In deference to Heidegger and for the sake of convenience, "philosophy" in this book is shorthand for "Western philosophy." I briefly return to the question of the relationship between Western and non-Western philosophical traditions at the end of the book.

In ordinary usage, the word "philosophy" has come to take on a range of meanings. As an adjective, for example, "philosophical" usually denotes resignation or acceptance regarding some unfortunate situation. For example, the coach of a sports team might be philosophical about her team's loss, meaning that she is thoughtful or stoic in the fact of her team's loss. But while the practice of philosophy tends to be introspective and dispassionate, philosophers are not always necessarily detached and emotionally uninvolved in their concerns. Indeed, history is dotted with stories of people, such as Socrates, who wittingly or unwittingly paid for their philosophical convictions with their lives.

"Philosophy" can also refer to a set of principles. Corporations sometimes make mention of their philosophies regarding production or customer service. An automaker, for example, might refer to its design philosophy in its advertising. What advertisers aim to do in such cases is to inform consumers about the guiding principles or values behind their goods or services. They want to let the public know "where they're coming from," so to speak. This gets a little closer to what philosophy means in its most general sense, but it still leaves much unsaid about philosophy as a field of study.

A typical dictionary entry defines "philosophy" along the lines of an inquiry into the fundamental principles of reality, human knowledge, reasoning, logic, values, and the mind. Specific definitions vary from one dictionary to another, but most of them make reference to some or all of the above concepts. Such definitions are fine as far as they go, but dictionaries are in the business of providing quick and handy definitions rather than delving into debates about meaning. Reaching a consensus about the meaning of "philosophy," then, turns out to be not as straightforward for philosophers as it is for lexicographers. Philosophers have competing conceptions about the meaning of what it is they do and what philosophy is about. We briefly survey some of these conceptions next.

SOME COMPETING CONCEPTIONS OF PHILOSOPHY

In this section I outline a number of competing conceptions about the nature of philosophy, and I question the idea that a single, over-arching definition can capture the essence of philosophy. At this point, a quick glance at the history of Western philosophy will be helpful.

Broadly speaking, there have been three main stages in the history of Western philosophy. The first, dating back to the Pre-Socratics, was marked by a preoccupation with metaphysical questions—that is, questions about the general nature of reality. The second phase, which was dominated by a succession of brilliant thinkers beginning with René Descartes (1596–1650), saw a shift from metaphysics as the dominant influence in philosophy to questions about the nature and possibility of knowledge about the world. And the third phase, which began early in the twentieth century, has seen philosophy fragment into roughly two schools: the analytic movement, where questions about the connections between logic, language, and the world assume center stage; and continental philosophy, which itself includes a host of areas such as the existential and postmodern movements. The general trend suggested by this very basic historical overview is that the level of confidence in our ability to establish unmediated contact with the world has waned over time, but it also reflects a heightened sensitivity to the importance of the methods involved in the practice of philosophy. This change in focus, from philosophical issues *per se* to the analysis of the linguistic and logical means by which we formulate our questions, has taken philosophy to new levels of complexity and technical sophistication, as we shall see in Chapter Three.

For some, philosophy is essentially an interactive and social activity. On this view, philosophy consists of dialogue arising between people about questions of a very general nature. We are misguided to expect philosophy to yield final, definitive answers to philosophical problems according to this interpretation of philosophy, since philosophy is an open-ended endeavor. Rather than conclude that philosophy is therefore an exercise in futility, we might as well accept this open-endedness as a cause for celebration. In his book *The Problems of Philosophy*, Bertrand Russell (1872–1970) powerfully evokes this sentiment, arguing that philosophy is to be valued not so much for the answers it produces, but for the enrichment we gain from the process of tackling philosophical questions. Pondering such questions, according to Russell, takes us beyond our everyday concerns, encourages us to tolerate the ideas of others, and expands our intellectual horizons.

Issues in philosophy are broad enough to encompass the foundations of both the liberal arts and the sciences. Moreover, progress in philosophy tends to be slow and hard-won if progress is made at all. Many of the debates about the nature of reality, knowledge, truth, and ethics initiated by ancient philosophers such as Plato and Aristotle (384–322 B.C.E.) endure to this day. This is apt to create the impression, especially for those new to the subject, that philosophy never makes progress and that it has a history of doing nothing but spinning its wheels. This perception is understandable and

8

to some extent justified, but I think it is too pessimistic because it overlooks the fact that philosophical problems are also eliminated from time to time. For instance, explaining electrical phenomena such as magnetism, lightning, and static electricity was for a long time a philosophical problem. Actually, it was both a scientific and philosophical problem, but these phenomena were observed long before there were any sharp distinctions between science and philosophy. The eventual success of Maxwell's theory of electromagnetism in unifying electrical and magnetic phenomena, and the further success of the modern electro-weak theory in unifying the electromagnetic and weak nuclear forces has seen electromagnetism disappear as a philosophical issue. Electrical and magnetic activity are now understood within the framework of quantum theory as manifestations of certain particles, radiation, and fields. Of course, if our current theories of basic physics should fail for one reason or another, the nature of electrical phenomena might once again become a philosophical issue, but suffice it to say that for now, electricity is no longer a problem for philosophers. Furthermore, it is easy to forget that questions such as whether the earth is round or whether all matter is made up of only four elements were once regarded as problems in natural philosophy. So while philosophy has no shortage of perennial problems, it is easy to lose sight of the gains we have made in understanding the world due to the efforts of those thinkers who have taken on philosophical problems.

Another sense in which physics models philosophy is that they both pursue a complete theory of the world, or *Theory of Everything* in the parlance of physics. Even if such a theory materializes, however, it would not follow from this that every question of interest to scientists and philosophers would automatically be answered, although many physicists and philosophers would then regard their work as having been done. The history of this conception of philosophy, which we might call the heroic quest for absolute truth, stretches back into antiquity, and the dream that philosophy might some day reveal final, general, and absolute truths about the world still casts a powerful spell over our imaginations. But this dream has very much soured in recent decades for a variety of reasons. Not the least of these reasons centers on a fascinating result in logic in 1931 due to Kurt Gödel (1906–78). Gödel proved that in certain formal systems, the true statements expressible in those systems outstrip our capacity to prove them, a result that in effect prevents us from ever fully circumscribing truth.

Having made some general comments about various conceptions of philosophy, there is still more to say about what exactly philosophy is and what motivates philosophers. Clearly, philosophy is, at least in part, a search for answers to questions about the nature of existence, knowledge, values, the human mind, logic, reasoning, and rationality. But not all philosophers concur that there are any legitimate philosophical questions. At one point in his career, the twentieth-century Austrian-British philosopher Ludwig Wittgenstein (1889–1951) rejected the idea that there are any meaningful philosophical questions. He didn't deny that we *think* there are philosophical questions, but he thought that these questions are pseudo-problems, confusions that arise due to misunderstandings about the way we use language. Once we clarify the meanings of key words used in framing traditional philosophical problems, he argued, so-called philosophical "problems" disappear. But to appropriate Mark Twain's *bon mot*, reports of philosophy's death are grossly exaggerated, and the irony here is that those who come to bury philosophy by purporting to show that it has died themselves contribute to ... you guessed it, philosophy! Suffice it to say that, at least for many of us, genuine philosophical problems *do* exist, problems that constitute legitimate and important areas of intellectual enquiry.

The pursuit of philosophy springs from the feelings of wonder, awe, and curiosity we experience when we begin to reflect upon the world around us. These experiences typically present themselves to us at an early age. Parents know too well that children are apt to pose surprisingly philosophical questions spontaneously and quite innocently, typically from about age five onward. Where do we come from? What happens to me when I die? Does Santa

Claus exist? These questions—even the last one—are all fascinating philosophical questions. For some, major changes such as births or deaths of family members, sudden career changes, or other significant events precipitate philosophical reflection. But while the urge to philosophize may stir within us as a response to such events, there is a big difference between the emotional responses we often experience in such situations, and the careful reflection of philosophy. It is to this end that the discipline and tools of philosophy are invaluable.

I have outlined a range of conceptions about philosophy but have so far said nothing about the approach I adopt in this book. Much of the material in the following pages is expository and descriptive in nature, but merely to talk about philosophy is not to philosophize, and is not nearly as interesting. I venture philosophical speculations of my own at various points throughout this book, especially in Chapter One and the concluding chapter. These speculations are in the tradition of the currently unfashionable heroic quest for absolute truth, although I hasten to add that for reasons I will return to later, this undertaking is at best open-ended and at worst hopelessly quixotic. Philosophy is, in a sense, greater than any of us; it is, to paraphrase Samuel Taylor Coleridge, a river that runs through caverns measureless to humans. But rather than despair at our inability to exhaust philosophy, or even its definition, we can rejoice at the prospect of the further discoveries awaiting us if we set sail down the river and into the sunlit sea.

I conclude this section with some comments on the qualities philosophers need to cultivate and the importance of philosophy. Tenacity, perseverance, patience, creativity, an appetite for straight thinking, and a willingness to follow arguments wherever they lead are all assets in philosophy. So is having an abiding curiosity about the world, boundless mental energy and humility enough to give up on one's philosophical labors and go back to square one. These remarks suggest that philosophy is, if nothing else, challenging. Is it ultimately a challenge worth taking up, or is philosophy in the final analysis an exercise in futility?

I refuse to believe that philosophy is futile, even if we never manage to resolve another philosophical question satisfactorily. Like Russell, I believe we derive intangible benefits from stretching ourselves in attempting to answer such questions. In a passage defending the importance of philosophy, G.K. Chesterton once wrote that not only does philosophy affect matters, it is the only thing that affects matters. And indeed, we should not underestimate the significance of philosophy in defining who we are and what we stand for. To invoke a distinction due to C.S. Lewis (1898–1963), philosophy is something that adds immeasurably to the value of survival, even if it has no obvious survival value.

STARTING POINTS

In setting out to solve a problem, whether it be an intellectual one or not, deciding where to start and how to go about solving the problem is critical, because one's point of departure can have a major impact on where one ends up and because effective problem-solving depends heavily on one's plan of action or methodology. These considerations are also relevant when it comes to starting out in philosophy, and in the case of philosophy they are intertwined in crucial and unique ways.

What starting points are available to us in our quest to understand the world in philosophical terms? If we are to arrive at any answers to our question at all, we obviously must start somewhere; the question of course is where? Unfortunately, in philosophy, unlike in the case of a real-world problem such as a car breakdown, we are on our own and have nothing to guide us other than whatever questions and problems strike us as worth investigating. We may read the works of other philosophers or talk to them to find out what they are interested in, but to engage in philosophy means not contenting oneself with the authority of others, no matter how famous or influential they may be. Not only does no one have the final answers to the deepest questions about our existence, but worse still, no one even really knows where to look for the answers or how best to go about finding them. In this sense, philosophizing is like the conception of life identified by the postwar French philosophers called existentialists, who likened the human condition to finding ourselves in a sort of trackless expanse in which we do not have the benefit of fixed points or absolutes to guide us. We construct our lives as a series of choices, according to the existentialists, choices for which we alone bear responsibility. In starting out as philosophers, we similarly find ourselves on our own, forced to make key choices.

Having said that, however, one of the main themes of this book is that we face a choice between two fundamentally different starting points when we set out to tackle philosophical problems: an *objective* and a *subjective* starting point. The former assumes that there are objective answers to those problems and is grounded in the conviction that the world around us exists objectively; the latter makes no such assumptions about objective answers and an objective world and takes as its point of departure one's own immediate experience as a thinking, feeling subject. This choice and its implications reverberate throughout the book, but rather than defend either option at this point, I want to suggest that they loosely parallel two fundamentally different ways of doing philosophy, what are called philosophical methodologies.

Of the two major philosophical methodologies that roughly parallel the starting points mentioned above, the first stresses our ability to reason our way to solutions and presupposes that philosophical problems are amenable to rational analysis. This is the *rationalist* tradition, perhaps most famously exemplified by Plato. The other tradition downplays our powers of rationality and seeks instead to let our philosophizing be guided by whatever clues, experimental results, and observations that present themselves. This is the *empirical* approach, represented by Aristotle among many others. Actually, in real-world problem solving as well as in philosophy, we typically look for help wherever we can find it in developing solutions and answers, and so in practice the distinction between these two methodologies is not always clear cut. But they are nevertheless sufficiently different to demarcate two major traditions in the history of philosophy. Is there anything to guide us in choosing between rationalist and empiricist methodologies? Alas there isn't, because even the process of contemplating how to go about doing philosophy involves philosophizing; that is to say, deciding how to go about philosophizing is itself already a matter of practicing philosophy!

In the case of a real-world problem such as a car breakdown, distinguishing between starting points and methodologies is relatively easy. The event of a car breaking down, after all, presents itself as the obvious starting point of the problem. Diagnosing the problem and deciding what to do about it are different matters. As usual, though, things are not so straightforward in philosophy. Starting points and methodologies in philosophy are often intertwined, but my point here is that where one begins and how one proceeds crucially determine what sorts of answers one arrives at.

Whenever we engage in philosophy, deciding where to begin is absolutely crucial because one's point of departure may involve unjustified—or worse still, unjustifiable—assumptions, assumptions which might diminish the credibility of one's position. In other words, while philosophers aspire to "begin at the beginning," as it were, in addressing a philosophical problem, the difficulty, as I suggested above, is that there is no beginning to be found. For this reason, it is always important to be as explicit as possible about articulating one's assumptions in philosophy, especially if such assumptions are controversial, which they usually are. Doing so helps clarify "where we are coming from," so to speak, which in turn makes our philosophical positions more transparent. Good philosophers are always looking to further our understanding of issues without taking conventional assumptions for granted. And progress in philosophy ultimately depends upon our ability to look at old problems in new and fruitful ways—to find, in other words, new beginnings.

To summarize this section, I have argued that where we begin answering our question cannot be separated from how we proceed with our investigations. I also urged that we face a fundamental choice when we begin philosophizing—a choice between adopting an objective or a subjective starting point—and that this choice bears crucially on the sorts of answers we are likely to find.

ABOUT THE BOOK

For the purposes of this book, I have settled on the following as representing the main branches of philosophy: *metaphysics* and *philosophy of mind*, *logic* and *philosophy of language*, *epistemology* and *the nature of truth*, *ethics*, *philosophy of science*, and *philosophy of religion*. I devote whole chapters to these topics, but I must add that this taxonomy is neither exhaustive nor definitive. Gaping omissions abound; *aesthetics*, *social philosophy*, and *political philosophy*, for example, are all legitimate contenders for inclusion. And the many subjects I pay only scant attention to include the postmodern movement, semiotics, and feminist theory.

I freely admit to indulging my particular areas of interest in this book, and I do not pretend to be able to do justice to philosophy as a whole in these few pages. I should also add that I think attempts to impose hard and fast divisions between various areas of philosophy, or for that matter between philosophy and the rest of the arts and sciences, are arbitrary. For the most part, I have tried to keep the writing as accessible as possible. Two sections, however, stand apart from the rest of the book in terms of their level of accessibility and should be regarded as optional for introductory readers. They are § 3.6, in which I develop a moderately technical argument that, relative to certain assumptions, not everything is humanly knowable, and Chapter 7, where I draw together many of the themes of the book and summarize my position on a number of those themes. My hope is that you will find these sections to be stimulating rather than daunting or off-putting, and that you will at least find some interest in appreciating where one of your fellow travelers currently stands in his quest to make sense of himself and the world around him.

CHAPTER I

Metaphysics:
The Nature of Existence

Let us contemplate existence.

— CHARLES DICKENS

1.0: INTRODUCTION

Metaphysics is an inquiry into the general nature of reality and, as far as we know, is the oldest of philosophical preoccupations in Western thought. So old and general are metaphysical questions, in fact, that they pre-date the word "metaphysics" itself, which was coined by an early editor of Aristotle's works. Questions about the abstract structure and nature of reality are numerous and have elicited a bewildering array of responses.

What sorts of questions do metaphysicians ask? The list is extensive, but here is a small sample of some traditional metaphysical problems: Does the world ultimately consist of just one thing or type of thing, or does it rather consist of many things or types of things? Is the world finite or infinite in extent? Is there a distinction between the way things appear to be and the way they really are? What is the nature of time? Do abstract entities such as numbers or concepts exist, and if so, in what sense? Is there a God or other supreme being? Is space continuous or discrete, and is it absolute or relational in nature? Do we have genuine free will in our actions, or are our actions and even thoughts all determined by factors such as laws of nature? Do we survive death and continue to exist as disembodied entities? In a world that seems to be constantly changing, does anything remain constant? Why is there something rather than nothing at all?

Incomplete as it is, the above list gives an indication of the enormous range of metaphysical topics. To reflect upon such questions is to realize just how difficult they are and how apt they are to raise further questions. For example, if we ask whether or not God exists, we first need to agree about exactly who or what it is we are talking about. Are we contemplating a real, physical entity, a state of mind, a moral concept, a creative force, the meaning of the word "God," or some combination of the above?

Metaphysics includes several subject areas: ontology, the study of being or existence; the question of free will versus determinism, which is concerned with whether we have genuinely free thoughts or actions; and the philosophy of mind, which is concerned with the nature of the mind and its place in the world. Connections abound between metaphysics and other areas of philosophy, and between the various subject areas within metaphysics; and our treatment of these and other topics in philosophy is piecemeal at best. We explore some of the major historical developments in metaphysics in the remainder of this chapter.

1.1: Metaphysics in Ancient Greek Philosophy

As far as we know from the rather sketchy direct evidence that survives, the earliest Western philosophers flourished on the Ionian coast in what is now western Turkey around 600 B.C.E. In the trading port of Miletus and the neighboring Mediterranean centers of Samos and Ephesus, a series of philosophers tried to explain the nature of the world in terms of a single *principle* or *primordial element* which they thought generates reality. Most of the candidates they proposed for this original element, or *arché*, as it was called, appear to us now with the benefit of hindsight to be quaint, while others show evidence of powerful and prescient thinking. Thales (*c.* 585 B.C.E.), who took the *arché* to be water, is an example of the former, while the atomists Leucippus (*c.* 440 B.C.E.) and Democritus (*c.* 460–370 B.C.E.), who developed surprisingly sophisticated theories of the world as consisting of indivisible particles moving around in a void, exemplify the latter. In any event, what is more important than the details of these early theories is what they signaled, which was the beginning of a new way of thinking about the world, a way based on observation and reason as opposed to the uncritical acceptance of superstition, dogma, authority or received wisdom. Above all, the invaluable legacy of these *Pre-Socratics*, as these Mediterranean philosophers are collectively known, is that they constructed *theories* about the world, albeit crude ones—theories which are open to discussion, modification and debate.

As I mentioned, Thales suggested that the *arché* is water, a theory actually not as naïve as it might seem at first, given the prevalence of water cults at that time in the harsh and arid Middle East. Thales was also no doubt keenly aware of the key role water plays in supporting life. And water has other special, chemical properties as well, such as the fact that, rare among naturally occurring substances, it is readily observed in nature in its solid, liquid, and gaseous forms.

Thales's successor, Anaximander (*c.* 612–545 B.C.E.), proposed that the *arché* is an abstract element known as the *apeiron*. Difficult to translate and still more difficult to conceptualize, the indefinite, formless, infinite *apeiron* was thought to somehow give rise to the world and its dualities, such as heat and cold, dryness and moisture, and so on. What is striking about Anaximander's theory is its level of abstraction, which sets it apart from many of the more prosaic, rival theories of the time. Competing theories tended to attribute *arché* either to individual elements such as Air, Fire, Earth or Water, or else, as in the more sophisticated theories of Empedocles (*c.* 495–435 B.C.E.) and Aristotle, to combinations of such substances.

One of the most important of the Pre-Socratics was the eponymous Pythagoras (*c.* 570–495 B.C.E.), whose theorem is familiar to anyone acquainted with high-school geometry. Pythagoras had such a deep fascination with the power of mathematics and the beauty of numbers that he went so far as to suggest that everything is a manifestation of numbers, an idea that has profoundly influenced thinkers from Plato to modern-day theoretical physicists, who aspire to explain the nature of the universe in terms of highly mathematical theories. The numbers Pythagoras had in mind, however, were *rational* numbers only—that is, ones that can be expressed in terms of ratios like ½, ¾, and so on. It is ironic that it was his own insights into the geometric properties of triangles that also led to the discovery—made not by Pythagoras himself, according to legend, but by a member of his school—of *irrational* numbers such as $\sqrt{2}$.

Another profound discovery Pythagoras made is that there is a correlation between the lengths of strings on stringed musical instruments and the tones they make when they are plucked, something that guitarists and violinists demonstrate every time they play their instruments. What's fascinating about this discovery is that while string lengths are continuous quantities, it turns out that aesthetically pleasing musical intervals such as fourths, fifths, and octaves correspond to whole number ratios of string lengths, which in the case of the above-mentioned intervals are 4:3, 3:2 and 1:2 respectively. This astonishing link between the arts and sciences and also between continuous and discrete quantities played a prominent role in Pythagoras's baroque and charming cosmology, which he based on the idea that the ordering principle of the cosmos is harmony. A legacy of this now largely forgotten theory is the expression "the music of the spheres."

The ideas of Parmenides (*c.* 510 B.C.E.) and Heraclitus (*c.* 500 B.C.E.) still reverberate in the Western world, and they form an intriguing study in opposites. Notorious even at the time for his cryptic writings, Heraclitus maintained that the world around us is subject to ceaseless change, a view encapsulated in his adage that we cannot step into the same river twice. What he meant is that since a river constantly changes, however quickly we re-enter a river it will have changed from what it was originally. But as a later commentator named Cratylus (late fifth century B.C.E.) realized, if we follow Heraclitus's reasoning to its logical conclusion, we could never step into the "same" river even once. The point Cratylus made was that if the world really is constantly changing, then nothing would remain fixed enough for a determinate object like a river to form in the first place! His argument is well taken, and it raises the problem of what, if anything, enables us to talk of the continued identity over time of objects that are subject to change, a problem answered in a radical way many centuries later, as we shall see later, by David Hume (1711–76). We take up the problem of change and identity in more detail in Chapter Five.

In stark contrast, Parmenides argued that reality is eternally unchanging, immovable, and unified, a philosophy summed up in that favorite mantra of mystics through the ages: All is One. But if All really is One and nothing, *contra* Heraclitus, ever really changes, how does Parmenides explain the glaring evidence that change seems to occur constantly? Are we really supposed to believe that falling rocks don't move or that we go nowhere when we go walking or jogging? Apparently so, since his famous pupil Zeno of Elea (*c.* 490 B.C.E.) tried to vindicate Parmenides in an ingenious series of paradoxes purporting to demonstrate the impossibility of motion, the indivisibility of spatial intervals and the unreality of the flow of time. A paradox arises when we are led to an apparently contradictory conclusion on the basis of what seem to be perfectly correct reasoning or assumptions.

A variation of one of Zeno's paradoxes implies that I cannot so much as even make my way out of the room I'm in. The reasoning is as follows. In order for me to leave the room, I first have to get to the door. But in order to get to the door, I first have to make it halfway to the door. In order to get to the halfway mark, however, I first have to get a quarter of the distance to the door. But before making it that far, I first have to get an eighth of the distance to the door, and so on *ad infinitum*. Zeno argues that this line of reasoning continues indefinitely, and that I would have to perform an infinite number of motions to get to the door. But it is not possible to perform an infinite number of tasks in a finite amount of time, according to Zeno, and so getting out of a room, and for that matter motion in general, is impossible! Zeno also concocted similar paradoxes to refute the idea that change and the passage of time are real.

Needless to say, not everyone is prepared to accept Zeno's conclusions, but his paradoxes have proved to be remarkably resilient and continue to challenge every new generation of mathematicians, physicists, and philosophers. Mathematicians and philosophers have tried to refute these paradoxes once and for all, resorting to ever more advanced mathematical techniques to do the job, the latest of which is called non-standard analysis. But there are some, including me, who remain unconvinced that this latest mathematical twist represents the final word in the history of efforts to dispose of Zeno's paradoxes. We will revisit Parmenides, Heraclitus, and Zeno's paradoxes in Chapter Five.

Parmenides was an old man by the time he traveled to Athens to debate his theory of reality with Socrates, an exchange reconstructed by Plato in a difficult but absorbing dialogue that bears Parmenides's name. Parmenides draws our attention to the notion that appearances—that is, the way things seem to be— are different from reality—the way things really are. This problem was to occupy a central place in Plato's writings, and it is as relevant a problem as ever. Consider the way our perceptions shift when we stare at the duck-rabbit image and Necker cube pictured below, which are familiar to readers of introductory psychology textbooks (see Figure 1). Think also of the way a straight rod appears to change shape when it is partially submerged in water, or how on a hot day the horizon in a desert shimmers like a lake. And if magicians were unable to fool our senses, they would soon be out of work. These examples go to show that we must

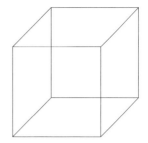

FIGURE I

abandon the idea that there is any simple, direct identification between objects in the world as they appear to us, and what the world is really like. But if reality really does differ from how it appears to us, what then can we say with confidence about the true nature of reality?

Plato made much of the appearance-reality distinction in his philosophy, and it played a key role in his subtle and sophisticated theory of reality based on entities he called Forms (*eidos*). In simple terms, Plato's idea is as follows. Some objects have certain features in common. For example, cats have whiskers in common; elephants have tusks and trunks in common; houses have entrances in common, and so on. Now, what is it that enables us to identify, for example, many different, individual cats or representations of cats—such as alley cats, Persian cats, drawings of cats, Sylvester the cartoon cat, and so on—as cats? One response might be to say that we learn to do so. Fine, but how can a child whose only previous exposure to cats is the household tabby, easily identify, say, the cartoon character Sylvester *as a cat*? After all, Sylvester has no fur and is not three-dimensional. Plato would account for this and other such feats of recognition in terms of our implicit awareness that all real cats and even representations of cats share, or participate in, a universal, abstract Form of "cathood" (or "catness"). It is their commonalities that unite cats and their representations and enable us to recognize many different, particular things, living or non-living, material or non-material, as cats. Having said that, not every cat or cat representation is necessarily a paradigm example of cathood. By the same token, for Plato it is the existence of a universal Form of Beauty that enables us to identify great works of art, music, and gorgeous scenery as beautiful, notwithstanding the many specific ways in which pieces of art, music, and nature differ.

For Plato, Forms extend beyond objects as we experience them; they are not simply a matter of common features or resemblances between things; and they are no mere concepts or definitions. Not only do they help make sense of the way we unify our experiences, they are very much real. Not only that, but Plato insists that in their abstract perfection, it is Forms, not the impermanent, short-lived, and ephemeral objects inhabiting the world around us, which lay true claim to existence. But if these abstract Forms are more real than ordinary, everyday objects, exactly what and where can they be? After all, we only ever see and experience individual cats or their representations, not some entirely abstract, ideal cat. Plato argued that Forms inhabit a realm beyond the physical domain, but he thought that we can access this realm if we dedicate ourselves to the task sufficiently, a challenge he regarded as a sort of Holy Grail for philosophers.

Plato's theory of Forms has much to be said for it. In his defense, note first that in accepting the reality of another level of existence, Plato's theory is perfectly consistent with religions such as Christianity—which incidentally was heavily influenced by Platonism—and Hinduism, which holds that the everyday world is a veil of illusion, called *maya*. Interestingly, Plato also believed in the immortality of the soul and in reincarnation. Secondly, there are powerful reasons to suppose that not everything that exists is directly perceived or experienced. Public opinion, interest rates, integrity, justice, credibility, charm, pessimism, and many other things are not perceived in the same way we perceive apples and oranges, but they can nevertheless affect us in very real ways, and all of them are arguably real in one way or another.

Plato gave pride of place in his otherworldly realm to the Forms of abstract concepts such as Truth, Beauty, and Justice, and he regarded Good to be a kind of ultimate Form. And in a world prone to change, error, and uncertainty, it is not implausible to suppose that at least some things, somehow, somewhere, remain constant. The truths of mathematics and logic are prime candidates for such immutable entities, and in fact Plato believed in the eternal existence of these truths. For all their invisibility and intangibility, it may be, ironically, that the existence of such thoroughly abstract objects as Forms is actually required to make sense of the mundane world of cabbages and kings.

On the other hand, Plato's theory leaves itself open to various criticisms. For example, it does nothing to account for much of what we know, or at least what we *think* we know. Any knowledge we have of the world around us that comes to us via our senses, such as my conviction that I am currently typing words on a computer keyboard, must ultimately be illusory as far as Plato is concerned, since all such perceptions belong to the realm of appearances. But surely this is hard to swallow. How could I possibly be mistaken about my belief that I am currently typing words on a computer; and how could you possibly be wrong to think you really are reading these same words? This is a problem Descartes was to confront many centuries later, as we shall see in Chapter Three.

Plato's most celebrated student was Aristotle, who lived at a time when Athens was already heading into decline. Nevertheless, Aristotle's body of work represents perhaps the crowning achievement of the ancient Greeks. Whereas Plato sought ultimate reality in a realm beyond the world around us, Aristotle strove to "reify" metaphysics, that is, ground it in the everyday world that Plato disdained as standing between ourselves and true reality. Aristotle was a prototypical scientist, and it is no overstatement to say that his talent for classification is unrivaled in the history of science and philosophy. The first person ever to apply the concepts of genus and species to living things, he effectively launched the field of biology single-handedly. And his ideas about physics, while they have not withstood the test of time as well as some of his other contributions, were woven into a monumental philosophical system that continued to dominate Western thought for over two thousand years. To medieval philosophers, he was known simply as "the Philosopher." But Aristotle's staggering talents did not end there, and his writings on ethics and syllogistic logic, a subject he also invented, hold their own to this day.

Aristotle sought in his metaphysics to focus on objects as they present themselves to us, which he called the study of Being as Being, rather than invoke some domain beyond the everyday world. What, then, is the nature of a thing such as a cat? Aristotle's point of departure is the distinction between quantity and quality. This distinction correlates closely with substance, which pertains respectively to things that exist "on their own," so to speak, and attribute, which refers to the properties of things. Substances are primary beings, meaning that they have their own natures and enjoy independent existence. For instance, cats, people, apples, trees, and stars are substances, according to Aristotle, whereas a table is not, because its existence is ancillary to whoever made it. Moreover, a cat can exist without its whiskers, but the existence of whiskers is dependent on cats, which for Aristotle indicates that a cat is a primary being, whereas whiskers are not.

So far so good, but what distinguishes one substance from another? Aristotle's answer to this makes use of a distinction between essential and accidental properties. Essential properties are those attributes that are required to identify an individual *as* an individual, whereas an accidental property is one that an individual can relinquish and yet remain the same individual. For example, it is an essential feature of Wayne Gretzky that he is human, but an accidental feature of him that he wears his hair short; he could grow his hair out instead, shave it off altogether, lose it all in his old age, and so on. Along with Plato, Aristotle was also concerned with the idea of form, but Aristotle's conception of form was very different from Plato's. A lump of putty is made of matter, but it can assume any number of forms, and substance, for Aristotle, is a combination of matter and form. This distinction allowed Aristotle to explain change, which he thinks of as resulting from matter assuming different forms, a theory that elegantly reconciles the opposing views of Parmenides and Heraclitus on Being and Becoming.

It is probably no coincidence that the distinction between quantity and quality, and also between substance and attribute, reflects the subject-predicate structure shared by ancient Greek and many modern-day Western languages. The sentence *Grass is green*, for example, contains the noun "grass" as its subject term and the predicate, "is green," which refers to a property or attribute of grass. Of course, we no longer regard grass as a substance in the same way that Aristotle did, but what is interesting here is to consider the ways in which the form of language, reality, and philosophy might influence each other. I will have more to say about this complex issue in Chapter Two.

Finally, Aristotle thought that it is part of the essence of a substance to be disposed to behave in certain ways. Thus, it is in the nature of an apple seed to develop into an apple tree given an environment conducive to tree growth, and, less plausibly, it is the tendency of heavy objects literally to gravitate to where they are supposed to be, which is at the center of the earth. Everything has its place, or purpose, in his account of nature, a postulate Aristotle gave the status of a cosmic principle which he called the final cause (or *telos*) of things. To explain the function or essential nature of something in terms of its purpose is known as a teleological explanation. Various versions of this powerful and appealing metaphysical principle have drawn support through the ages. In biology, the teleological explanations of Aristotle held sway until the advent of Darwin's theory of natural selection, which obliges us to believe that evolutionary processes are blind. And in an altogether different context, pioneers of the American West who preached the theory of manifest destiny were espousing what is essentially a teleological doctrine.

Much is missing from this very brief survey of the metaphysics of the ancients, most regrettably a discussion of Plato's mentor, Socrates. However, let us conclude this overview of metaphysics by fast-forwarding to what philosophers refer to as the early modern period.

1.2: METAPHYSICS IN THE EARLY MODERN PERIOD

The decline of the great, ancient civilizations of Greece and Rome also signaled a temporary decline in the vigor of Western intellectual life, but a series of outstanding Islamic scholars, including Avicenna (Ibn Sīnā, 980–1037) and Averroës (Ibn Rushd, 1126–98), kept learning in the arts and sciences alive, and also made valuable contributions to Aristotelian scholarship. Philosophical activity during the medieval period did not so much cease, however, as retreat to the monasteries of continental Europe and Britain, where the focus of philosophical debates turned to logic, abstruse debates in theology and the interpretation of Aristotle. Pre-eminent among philosophers of this period were St Anselm (1033–1109), who held the post of Archbishop of Canterbury; St Thomas Aquinas (1225–74), whose Christian reconstruction of Aristotle still forms the basis of orthodox Catholic theology; and Duns Scotus (1266–1308).

Thomism, as the system of Aquinas is called, dominated the philosophical agenda in Europe until the arrival of Descartes, who is widely regarded as having ushered in modern philosophy. A physiologist, physicist, and mathematician as well as philosopher, Descartes would be remembered today on the strength of his contributions to mathematics alone, of which the most important was his synthesis of algebra with geometry to create analytic geometry. Like Pythagoras and Plato before him, Descartes found in mathematics a level of rigor and precision he wanted to see in philosophy as well, and he attempted to secure philosophy on comparably firm foundations. His metaphysical system is laid out in three major works: *Principles of Philosophy*, the *Discourse on the Method*, which was originally a preface to a tract on optics, meteorology, and geometry, and his famous *Meditations*, which is still studied by every new generation of philosophy students. Reading Descartes, we find an excellent example of a philosopher aspiring to "begin at the beginning" by deliberately rejecting as many assumptions as he could. In his case, this involved questioning the origins of his knowledge and rejecting any knowledge he thought was potentially unreliable.

Descartes's ontological point of departure was his conception of substance, a pre-occupation of Aristotle's, and, in the form of *arché*, of the Pre-Socratics as well. Like Aristotle, Descartes sanctioned a fundamental distinction between dependent beings—those that require some other being for their existence—and independent beings, which exist autonomously. Some independent beings or substances are material, physical beings, but in addition Descartes theorized that some material entities, specifically human beings, are endowed with non-material minds. The minds of humans thus form a third ontological category for Descartes.

The fundamental distinction Descartes drew between mind and matter sparked a vigorous debate in metaphysics that endures to this day. Many people still regard the idea that we comprise a physical body and a non-physical mind as eminently plausible, and it has the added attraction of leaving the door open to Christian and other conceptions of an afterlife. Since Descartes regarded the mind's existence to be independent of the body's, it is perfectly reasonable to suppose on the basis of this view that a person's mind can continue to exist after her body is reduced to ashes and dust. The main problem for a so-called Cartesian dualist, however, is to explain how it is that mind and matter are supposed to interact. A cause-and-effect interaction between physical entities is one thing, but how is it that non-physical minds bring about physical changes? If my desire for a popsicle, for example, is something non-physical, then how does that desire manage to move my body to the freezer, open the freezer door, and bring the popsicle to my mouth? Descartes hypothesized that the pineal gland, a tiny gland at the base of the brain, functions as a sort of conduit through which the mind acts on the body. Precisely how and why this particular gland is the seat of the soul, however, was something he never managed to explain satisfactorily.

The nature of substance and the mind-body interaction problem were to become predominant concerns of leading philosophers for centuries to follow, particularly on the Continent. Notable among these philosophers were Baruch Spinoza (1632–77), Nicolas Malebranche (1638–1715), and Gottfried Wilhelm Leibniz (1646–1716). Malebranche suggested that minds and bodies are both real, but that they lead separate, parallel existences which are coordinated by God, who intervenes in the world as the need arises to make it appear as if the mind acts on the body.

For his part, Leibniz met these problems by advancing an intricate ontology based on atomic entities he called monads. Infinite in number, each monad is at the same time unique and inert with respect to every other one. Leibniz departed from the materialistic tradition of the ancient Greek atomists by postulating that these simple substances are immaterial; they resemble miniature souls. Moreover, each one of these living monads is a kind of microcosmic reflection of the entire universe, an idea reminiscent of William Blake's immortal line about beholding infinity in a grain of sand. As to how this vast mosaic of monads is integrated, Leibniz tells us that God specifically chose to create the particular collection of monads that we happen to experience as reality. The perfect integration of this collection of monads is known as the doctrine of *pre-established harmony*. On this account the problem of mind-body interaction does not arise, because for Leibniz there is no basic distinction between the physical and mental. This radical ontological pluralism contrasts starkly with the monism of Parmenides, for whom Reality consists of just one thing, but a more subtle version of Parmenidean monism was advanced by Leibniz's older contemporary, Baruch Spinoza.

Spinoza also denied that mind and matter are separate, arguing instead that the world is made of only one substance, but that this substance manifests itself in infinitely many ways, or attributes, mind and matter being but two such attributes. Mind and body are thus like two facets of a substance with infinitely many facets, a philosophy of mind referred to as dual-aspect theory. Spinoza claimed that this one substance goes by two names: God or Nature (in Latin: *Deus, sive Natura*), a theory that implies that God is literally immanent in everything. Moreover, what exists has always existed. Taken together, these claims mean not only that God did not create the universe, but that He exists in sinners no less than in saints, in garbage heaps no less than in holy water. Nothing is left to chance in Spinoza's cosmological picture; everything that occurs does so of strict necessity, the cause of everything being God. This position amounts to a form of pure determinism. As innocuous, if albeit highly speculative, as these metaphysical ideas might strike us today, Spinoza's beliefs were considered sufficiently heretical at the time to have him thrown out of the synagogue and his works banned.

Meanwhile in England, the stunning success of the materialistic, mechanistic worldview of Pierre Gassendi (1592–1655), Francis Bacon (1561–1626), and Descartes was winning converts among philosophers as well as the newly emerging fraternity of scientists. Foremost among philosophers in this milieu was John Locke (1632–1704), who, starting from direct experience, developed a philosophical system so intuitively appealing that in broad outline it still enjoys considerable currency today. According to the mechanistic worldview, we inhabit a world of material particles that are subject to physical forces. Locke supplemented this physical picture with a general account of matter, our knowledge, and our place in nature. In his description of matter, Locke made use of a distinction between two different kinds of qualities: primary qualities and secondary qualities.

Primary qualities, including solidity, shape, and extension, are those properties that are within, or intrinsic to, material bodies. Secondary qualities, on the other hand, which include colours, sounds, tastes, and smells, are not intrinsic to bodies, but rather are produced in us by the primary qualities of the microscopic constituents of bodies. That is to say, primary qualities have *powers* to produce in us experiences of secondary qualities. What is interesting about this is that, like Plato, Locke postulated a difference between the way things really are and the way they appear to us to be, but Locke's account is more sophisticated than Plato's. As for how we interact with the world, Locke thought that the external world and its contents impinge upon our senses, which in turn produce ideas in our minds. Details about how ideas arise are a matter of physiology, a reasonable enough suggestion and one that might lead you to regard Locke's theory as more plausible than many of the others we have encountered so far!

The main problem with Locke's system is that he has to allow that we don't have direct contact with the outside world; strictly speaking we are acquainted only with our sensations, and, as Locke conceded, the correspondence between such impressions and objects is only partial at best. For Locke, sensations like tastes and smells are supposedly the effects of powers inherent in objects, but they are also features of human psychology, and thus they are arguably not intrinsic features of objects themselves. This difficulty was exploited by the Irish Anglican bishop George Berkeley (1685–1753), who rejected Locke's primary-secondary quality distinction along with the notion of powers, insisting that Locke's claims have no basis whatsoever in our actual experience.

Berkeley agreed with Locke that we directly experience only our sensations, but Berkeley thought that to go further than this and assert that those sensations somehow originate in something entirely different—material objects—was unjustified. Thus Berkeley arrived at a metaphysical position according to which objects and sensations exist to the extent that they are perceived. The thrust of Berkeley's theory is succinctly rendered in Latin as *esse est percipi* (to be is to be perceived). This radical doctrine would seem to imply that whenever, for example, I fall asleep and no one else is in the room, my bed ceases to exist unless I immediately start dreaming about my bed, and that a tree falling in a remote forest makes no sound if no one is there to hear its fall. However, Berkeley resisted this conclusion—some feel all too conveniently—by asserting that God not only watches over beds and falling trees in the absence of humans, but has all the other experiences required to "prop up" otherwise unobserved parts of the world when we are nowhere to be found. Although there is more depth and subtlety to Berkeley's theory than this highly sketchy account would indicate, it is nevertheless true to say that, for better or worse, Berkeley's system has never attracted a very large following.

Extreme as it is, Berkeley arrives at his metaphysical position with careful, sober steps in the course of his critique of Locke's ostensibly reasonable philosophy. But if his conclusions are unpalatable, where does he go wrong? Perhaps the root of this dilemma is our expectation that we are capable of adducing solutions to metaphysical problems at all. If the answers we arrive at are absurd, maybe this says more about our own intellectual abilities and limitations than it does about the veracity of our metaphysical ideas. Maybe, in other words, it just so happens that we are better at asking metaphysical questions than we are at answering them. The great Scottish philosopher David Hume, who regarded metaphysical claims of the sort Locke and Berkeley entertained to be fruitless, inclined to this view.

Two prominent targets of Hume's compelling critique were the concepts of identity and causality. In the case of identity, Hume realized that we have a natural inclination to believe that objects such as trees exist continuously over time. But closer analysis, according to Hume, reveals that our experience of a tree consists in nothing more than a series of tree-like impressions, from which we *infer* that the tree exists continuously over time. Hume did not deny that the notion of identity plays a central role in the way we structure and co-ordinate our experiences. Rather, his point was to deny that identity is something over and above our impressions; it is something we confer upon objects rather than something that exists in objects themselves.

Similar considerations apply to causal (as opposed to casual!) relations, which for Hume are everything to do with our psychological makeup and nothing to do with objective relations between events in a world beyond our minds. The purpose of a theory of causality is to explain the relationship between causes and effects, and how this relationship differs from phenomena such as correlations and coincidences. Understanding the differences among these phenomena has many practical and important implications. Suppose, for example, that researchers discover that there is a strong positive correlation between the consumption of bananas and the incidence of bone cancer. In this case we would definitely want to know whether there is something in bananas that causes bone cancer; whether the correlation is due to some other underlying cause that just so happens to be prevalent among banana-eaters; or whether the researchers have merely stumbled upon a strange coincidence. Causes are commonly conceived to be real, physical mechanisms, but on Hume's account, they are merely a matter of certain patterns and regularities that manifest themselves in our experience, and are not to be found in the world itself. On the basis of the recurring patterns in our experience, we form conclusions about how the world works and what it is like. For example, on the basis of our experiences of letting go of heavy objects, we come to conclusions about how they behave and eventually generalize these conclusions under the rubric of laws of gravity. Such conclusions are called *inductive generalizations*, and their applications permeate not only science, but our everyday decision making as well. Hume argued that such generalizations constitute the very idea of causality and laws of nature, reasoning that while we may come to expect certain phenomena to repeat themselves in predictable ways, none of this is a matter of logical necessity. Hume thought that no amount of experimenting with apples to see what happens when we drop them is sufficient to guarantee that the next time we let go of a given apple, it will fall to the ground. This difficulty, which is known as Hume's problem of induction, vexes philosophers of science to this day.

Making choices and coming to decisions seem to be pervasive aspects of the human condition, and most of us believe that at least some of the time we are genuinely free to choose between alternatives when we make choices and act on them. Should I go to work or phone in sick? Should I turn in that lost wallet as I found it or keep the cash? Should I order a tasty burger or stick to my diet and order a salad instead? Should I take a left or right turn at the next intersection? Some of these choices are more important than others, and some of them have decidedly moral implications. On the other hand, it is not uncommon to feel that what happens to us in life is beyond our ability to control, and that coming to terms with this is the road to inner peace and calm. One argument in support of this view is that all our thoughts and actions are determined, either by some supreme being, by other outside forces such as laws of nature, or by something else altogether. The idea that our lives might be entirely at the mercy of physical forces and the laws of nature gained considerable credibility with the rise of science in the seventeenth and eighteenth centuries. The enormous successes scored by scientists and philosophers such as Galileo, Newton, and Descartes in explaining the workings of the world in material and mechanical terms culminated in the emergence of a new worldview, or paradigm, according to which the universe resembles one vast machine. The French astronomer Pierre Simon de Laplace (1749–1827) articulated this vision of a comprehensively deterministic cosmos, but if this worldview holds for everything in the world, ourselves included, then where, if at all, does human free will fit into the picture? This is the problem of free will versus determinism.

With respect to this problem, Hume ventured the view that free will and determinism are in fact compatible, by which he meant that on the one hand our thoughts and actions flow freely from our characters and dispositions, but that these characters and dispositions are themselves determined. What he means by this is that our actions are in general neither random nor capricious, and that our decisions, while freely arrived at, are also informed by the regularities that we observe in the world and rely upon to achieve our aims. We avoid getting too close to open flames, for example, because we have come to associate getting too close to them with pain and burns. In this case, our choice to avoid fires is, according to Hume, both freely arrived at and also conditioned by our past experience of fires. For Hume there is in principle no contradiction between freely choosing some course of action and the idea that this choice has a detailed explanation. While not everyone is persuaded by Hume's attempt to reconcile free will and determinism, it remains an attractive option to many current players in the field. In Chapter Four we return to the relevance to ethics of this problem.

Hume's metaphysical results—or rather the lack of them— evince a particularly potent expression of skepticism. We will discuss skepticism more fully in Chapter Three, but note for now that a skeptic is someone who rejects the possibility of certain knowledge. Although Hume was by no means the first skeptic— several schools of skepticism had already flourished among the ancient Greeks—some philosophers have found Hume's arguments to be irresistible. Hume's skeptical outlook also extended to the philosophy of religion, where his clever rebuttals of some famous arguments for the existence of God still provide powerful ammunition for non-believers, although Hume himself was circumspect enough not to publish his heretical views about God and Christianity during his lifetime.

1.3: METAPHYSICS IN CONTEMPORARY PHILOSOPHY

We now take another arbitrary leap forward, this time to the beginning of the twentieth century. Unquestionably the most influential figure in philosophy in the period between Hume and the present was Immanuel Kant (1724–1804), of whom more in Chapter Three, although the iconoclastic and erratic genius Freidrich Nietzsche (1844–1900), whose devastating critiques of Christianity and traditional metaphysics shook philosophy to its foundations, also deserves special mention. Kant cast a shadow that extended over generations of German and other Continental philosophers, including Johann Gottlieb Fichte (1762–1814), Friedrich Schelling (1775–1854), Arthur Schopenhauer (1778–1860) and, most famously, G.W.F. Hegel (1770–1831).

Hegel's sprawling metaphysical system is predicated on the concept of *dialectic*, which is a process he uses to explain history and human thought. In Hegel's philosophy of process, change consists in the dynamic tension between dialectical elements he called *thesis* and *antithesis*, a tension that resolves itself in the creation of a *synthesis*. At this point the whole cycle begins anew, as every *synthesis* in turn becomes a *thesis*. This continuously evolving process culminates in the emergence of the *Absolute Spirit*, the point at which, according to Hegel, we become aware of the nature of the entire cosmos.

Hegel's philosophy dominated German philosophy in his day and was enjoying strong support in England at the dawn of the twentieth century until two young English philosophers, G.E. Moore (1873–1958) and Bertrand Russell, dissatisfied with what they saw as the metaphysical excesses of Hegel, initiated a revolution that was to become known as *analytic philosophy*. Analytic philosophy still prevails as the dominant philosophical school of thought in much of Great Britain, North America, Scandinavia, and Australasia. In general terms, analytic philosophers are concerned with spelling out the nature of the relationships between language and the world, where "language" encompasses both natural languages and the formal languages of mathematics and logic. Whereas Moore admonished us not to lose sight of common sense in our metaphysical pursuits, Russell adopted a more technical approach, aiming to clarify traditional metaphysical problems by way of searching analyses of language and logic. In the next chapter we shall explore some of these issues in greater detail.

These developments fed the emergence of an exacting and uncompromising movement known as *logical positivism*, which originated in Vienna in the 1920s and was promoted by Rudolf Carnap (1891–1970) and A.J. Ayer (1910–89), among others. Positivists, as its adherents were known, sought to banish from philosophy all metaphysical claims, which they took to be little more than meaningless speculation. Their criterion for adjudicating such issues was the *principle of verifiability*. Briefly, this principle stipulates that sentences are meaningful only to the extent that they are verifiable, which more or less restricts philosophy to logic and the empirical methods of the sciences, an outlook reminiscent of a stance that Hume had earlier prescribed. This philosophical movement, however, ironically fell victim to its own austerity, since any claim or argument one may mount in its defense itself falls foul of the verifiability principle. In other words, logical positivism's rejection of metaphysical claims is itself predicated on metaphysical presuppositions, and so logical positivism came to be seen as fatally flawed. A successor to this deflationary approach to metaphysics is the *descriptive metaphysics* of P.F. Strawson (1919–), who urged that we limit metaphysical talk to describing the structure of our thinking about the world, a strategy that effectively relegates metaphysics to the realm of psychology. Descriptive metaphysics may be contrasted with speculative metaphysics, which involves the construction of general theories about the nature of reality.

The influence of logical positivism had waned substantially by the middle of the twentieth century, although a proclivity for situating metaphysical problems in the philosophy of language still persists in Anglo-American philosophy. One leading practitioner of this approach to philosophy was Ludwig Wittgenstein, one of the foremost philosophers of language of the last century. Employing a pithy, at times almost impenetrable, writing style, he expounded a position called *logical atomism* in his first book, the *Tractatus Logico-Philosophicus*. In this work he reduces reality to atoms he calls *facts*, which have counterparts in the form of abstract *propositions*. Propositions are not to be confused with ordinary sentences, but are rather what those sentences express. As we shall see in the next chapter, propositions are very useful when it comes to explaining how sentences in different languages can express the same idea. According to Wittgenstein, facts and propositions share a common logical form, which explains how language manages to "picture" reality.

But Wittgenstein abandoned this theory of the connection between language and reality later in his career, focusing his attention instead on the various ways in which language is used. He came to understand language in essentially social terms and as a *tool*, or game, a development that sparked interest for a short time in what was called ordinary language philosophy. Now all but forgotten, the original aim of this program was to resolve philosophical debates through careful analyses of the ways in which key words in those debates function in language.

In recent years, metaphysics has made something of a comeback, even within analytical philosophy circles. This is due in some degree to the philosophical problems raised by the branch of physics known as quantum theory, which seems to challenge the traditional and intuitively plausible theory known as *metaphysical realism*. I shall have much more to say about metaphysical realism later, but for now it is enough to note that it is the view that the world exists independently of human observers. Impetus for the renaissance of metaphysics has also come from the unlikely direction of the analysis of sentences called *counterfactuals*. Counterfactuals are contrary-to-fact conditional sentences such as these:

If it weren't for television, the birth rate would be higher.

If fish had anchors instead of fins, they would sink.

The American philosopher David Lewis (1941–2001) argues that the best way to analyze counterfactuals involves taking seriously the existence of a multitude of real, possible worlds, in some of which, for example, fish really do have anchors for fins and they really do sink! However, the jury is still out on whether Lewis's arguments provide sufficient motivation for buying into his extravagant ontology of endless other worlds.

Another highly active research area in contemporary metaphysics is the philosophy of mind. Whereas Descartes thought that mind is a kind of non-physical substance and Hume thought of it as consisting in impressions and ideas, a range of alternative theories concerning the nature of the mind have surfaced in recent decades. Some of these theories have been driven by trends in psychology, while other theories have looked to the physical sciences, neuroscience, and the theory of computation for ways to explain the nature of mind. Inspired by the work of the behavioral psychologists B.F. Skinner and J.B. Watson, some philosophers, most notably Gilbert Ryle (1900–76), denied the existence of the mind as some sort of non-physical entity, identifying a mental state instead with its outward manifestation as behavior. Behaviorist psychologists and philosophers focused heavily on how human and animal subjects respond to external stimuli and how behavior can be conditioned by controlling those stimuli, but this program is now generally regarded as too limited to furnish the basis of a comprehensive theory of the mind.

A group of philosophers based in Australia, including D.M. Armstrong (1926–), J.J.C. Smart (1920–), and C.B. Martin (1924–), attempted to overcome the limitations of the behaviorist movement by positing a strict identification of mental states with certain physical states, specifically neural states. What is it to be in a given mental state? Identity theorists, as they are known, reply that it just is to be in a particular physical state. In other words, my craving for a popsicle is at the same time a certain state of my brain and nothing over and above that brain state. Identity theory hearkens back to some extent to the behaviorist school that preceded it, although Martin for one stresses that we must not lose sight of what it is like to have conscious experiences. His point is that while the taste of a luscious mango is indeed a matter of being in a certain brain state, that brain state has a certain *quality*, which consists of the experience of the person tasting the mango.

Identity theory in its original form appeared to rule out the possibility that other life forms with physiologies different from our own, such as aliens, or for that matter, computers, could have conscious experiences of the sort we have. Philosophers who take seriously the idea of artificial intelligence reject this conclusion, arguing that consciousness is a matter not so much of the physical makeup and activity of brains *per se*, but rather of the *functional organization* of the physical—or indeed even non-physical—system in question. Taking their lead from arguments formulated by the brilliant English mathematician Alan Turing (1912–54), these so-called functionalists dominated philosophy of mind during the 1970s and 1980s. However, support for their enterprise has slipped in recent years, due in part to mixed findings concerning the fitness of artificial intelligence as a model for the mind. Despite the intense level of activity in the field at present, no clear-cut alternative has emerged yet as a successor to this movement.

Analytic philosophy's preoccupation with logic, and its decidedly technical and scientific orientation, contrasts with the scene in twentieth-century continental metaphysics, where several major movements warrant brief mention. These include the phenomenological and existential schools associated with Edmund Husserl (1859–1938), Karl Jaspers (1883–1969), Heidegger, Jean-Paul Sartre (1905–80), and Maurice Merleau-Ponty (1908–61); the development of Freudian themes in the work of Jacques Lacan (1901–81); Hans-Georg Gadamer (1900–2002) and hermeneutics; and the postmodern camp led by Michel Foucault (1926–84) and Jacques Derrida (1930–). None of these movements is easily captured by quick summaries, but postmodernists seek to "deconstruct" texts and share an antipathy towards the notions of objectivity and objective truth in philosophy. Gadamer emphasizes the role of understanding and interpretation in our reading of texts, while phenomenologists and existentialists embrace human subjectivity as unavoidable and explore the consequences of this. This last group of philosophers contends that existence (or being) must be understood in terms of how it is given to us in conscious experience, and so philosophy itself becomes a kind of anatomy of consciousness. In addition, existentialists focus on the directness and immediacy of experience and on how the choices and decisions we must constantly make arise from the exigencies of the human condition.

Twentieth-century continental philosophy of language saw the development of a movement known as *semiotics*, which takes its lead from the structural linguistics of Ferdinand de Saussure (1857–1913). De Saussure construes language as being essentially a type of sign system. The role of language as a social instrument in shaping discourse, including philosophical discourse, is also a central theme for many European philosophers. Lacan analyzes the way in which language plays a part in structuring Freud's notion of the *unconscious*. Foucault, on the other hand, takes structuralist investigations further by exploring ways in which knowledge and power function as social institutions to produce, among other things, our conceptions of madness, sexuality, and social constructions of what is normal. In taking upon himself the task of deconstructing texts, Derrida challenges the idea that philosophers are able to transcend the linguistic and rhetorical conventions within which their writings are couched, and he attempts to describe how such limitations discredit the aims of traditional metaphysics. Deconstructionists conclude, among other things, that the meanings of texts are fluid rather than fixed, and that therefore texts are open to a plurality of readings and interpretations.

This brings to a close our short historical survey of metaphysics. You may be starting to sense by now the role that basic assumptions and starting points play in shaping the philosophies we have so far encountered. One such assumption is the idea that what exists is prior to, and independent of, what we know, and that therefore there is a real distinction between what there is— that is, metaphysics—and what we know—that is, epistemology. Objections to this assumption emerged, at least implicitly, as early as the time of the Pre-Socratics, when Protagoras (c. 490–c. 420 B.C.E.) proclaimed humans to be the measure of all things. But having acknowledged these assumptions, thorny questions remain for metaphysicians, such as those raised by Hume in questioning the extent to which metaphysical conclusions are contingent upon what we are capable of *knowing*.

We turn to these concerns in Chapter Three, where we investigate some of the connections between truth, metaphysics, and self-reference, but next we expand upon some other themes in this chapter, specifically the topics of language, logic, and truth.

CHAPTER 2

Logic:
Language, Reason, and Truth

Whereof one cannot speak, thereof one must be silent.

— LUDWIG WITTGENSTEIN

2.0: INTRODUCTION

In this chapter we explore a cluster of interconnected topics and problems concerning language, reason, argumentation, and truth, topics that for the sake of convenience I have gathered together under the rubric of logic. The main argument in this chapter, which I introduce in § 2.3, is that truth is not entirely reducible to language. I expand upon and further develop this theme in the next chapter. Although the argument I develop is not directly related to the passage from Wittgenstein that appears above, my conclusion is consistent with the sentiment he expresses.

We begin with a look at some of the characteristics, limitations, and peculiarities of language before turning to the nature of logic and its relationship to reason; and finally we discuss various conceptions of the nature of truth. The rise of analytic philosophy at the beginning of the twentieth century brought with it increased interest in all of these areas, and nowadays linguistic and semantic considerations are brought to bear upon virtually every area of philosophical research. Although we touch on only a few issues in logic and the philosophy of language, one of the main purposes of the discussion in this chapter is to impart a sense of the range, subtlety, and philosophical significance of two of the most important cognitive faculties available to us: our ability to reason and our ability to use language.

2.1: Reference, Meaning, and other Topics in the Philosophy of Language

Natural languages are the spoken, written or signed communication systems familiar to all of us because they pervade all human cultures. Examples of such languages, not all of which are still in use, include English, French, Swahili, Mandarin, Latin, Ligurian, American Sign Language (or Ameslan), and so on. In addition to natural languages, there are so-called *formal* languages, which perform specialized functions and tend to have strict rules of syntax. Formal languages are widespread in areas such as mathematics, logic, and computer programming. Beyond that, languages may be construed as situated within a broader context of sign and communication systems. Road signs, works of art, so-called body language, musical notation, and even music itself are all means by which we communicate, although the question of whether any such systems are languages *per se* is an area we will not venture into. There are more than enough philosophical problems raised by natural languages alone to occupy us for the remainder of this chapter; and from now on, we will use the word "language" to mean "natural language." In this section we explore a cluster of problems arising from language and its connection to the world around us.

Written languages reduce to components such as sentences, words, alphabet letters, characters, punctuation marks, and so on. In addition, linguists also study the sounds we utter in speaking languages, while grammarians focus on syntax and other structural characteristics of language. But as the medium through which we do most of our thinking, reasoning and philosophizing, understanding the structure, uses and limitations of language is of vital interest to researchers who study the workings of the mind, the nature of meaning, how words and sentences refer, rationality and cognition. Then there is the question of how language relates to the world at large, which is the central question of the third and most recent epoch in Western philosophy: analytic philosophy.

Let us begin by asking how words refer and how they acquire their meanings. The word "meaning" itself has many senses, but when it comes to words, we usually take the meaning of a word to be specified by its definition. Now we look up words in dictionaries to learn their definitions, but dictionaries are closed systems in the sense that all of the words we find in dictionaries are defined in terms of each other, and definitions do not take us beyond the pages of dictionaries. Another way of thinking about meaning is that words acquire meanings by referring to other, non-linguistic things. On this account, we coin words in order to name things in the world, and in the process we confer upon those words their respective meanings. The meanings of words become entrenched to the extent that words used for the purposes of naming gain currency throughout a community of language users. As obvious as this conception of meaning in terms of reference and naming might seem, it turns out to be fraught with difficulties. One problem is that the assumption that individual words or ideographs in a language are the basic unit of meaning is debatable. Naming words, such as nouns, pick out *specific objects*, such as my cat, your hat, and so on, and *types of objects*, such as mammals, water, gold, and so on, but just as an object can only be fully understood in the context of its relationships to other things, so, too, individual words are understood in the context of the larger linguistic structures, such as sentences, within which they are embedded. Theories of meaning (or semantics) that are more holistic in orientation take meaning to be a function of these larger linguistic structures. But there are other problems concerning meaning and reference, such as whether words and their meanings really reflect features of the world, or whether they rather have more to do with features of human psychology.

For reasons that will emerge in the next chapter, the idea that there is a world outside us that is fixed, determinate, and filled with objects waiting to be named and identified is hopelessly naïve. If so, however, this suggests that we play a role in identifying and constructing the objects that inhabit the world. And if this is so, it follows that there is an element of human subjectivity in the process of picking out objects in the world. This spells trouble for any reference theory of meaning. If one person thinks of a certain large mound of rocks as a hill and another person regards it as a mountain, who is right? And who is to say who is right? But there are other complications as well. The German philosopher Gottlob Frege (1848–1925) argued that a word or phrase does more than merely refer to, or pick out, some object. In addition to its reference (or *Bedeutung*), Frege thought that a word or phrase also has a certain connotation, which he called sense (or *Sinn*). The sense of the ancient name for the morning star, Phosphorus, is different from that of Hesperus, the name of the evening star, even though it turns out that both words refer to one and the same thing: the planet Venus. Similarly, the sense of the expression "the heartless thief who stole my wallet" differs totally from "my old high school buddy Dave," even though they may refer to one and the same person. In general, then, the meanings of words, phrases, and sentences involve more than simple reference.

Another problem with the idea that words and phrases simply name human-independent objects is that words and phrases can name things that don't exist. Unicorns, the tooth fairy and the president of Canada are all examples of names of non-existent entities. How can the notion of reference explain terms such as these? Bertrand Russell addressed this problem in his renowned *theory of descriptions*. A description employing the definite article "the" is a *definite description*, whereas one making use of an indefinite article such as "a" or "an" is an *indefinite description*. Russell denied that definite descriptions, such as "the book I am writing" and "the president of Canada," and indefinite descriptions, such as "a unicorn" and "an apple," refer to objects directly. Rather, he claimed that such terms have a complex logical structure which can be analyzed in such a way as to sidestep the notion of reference altogether. On Russell's account, the term "the president of Canada" turns out upon analysis to be "there is at least one thing that is the president of Canada and at most one thing that is the president of Canada," a description which happens not to coincide with anything that actually exists. (Just for the record, Russell used logical notation to express these descriptions, which in the case of our current example is: $\exists x \, [Px \, \& \, \forall y \, (Py \rightarrow y = x)]$, where P represents the property of being the president of Canada). By replacing the notion of reference with description, Russell's theory solves several other knotty problems of meaning and reference in addition to accounting for names of non-existent things. His work has been the subject of ongoing debate and refinement by Peter Strawson, Keith Donnellan (1931–), and John Searle (1932–), among others.

An alternative to Russell's descriptivist account of reference is the causal theory of reference, so called because it attempts to spell out reference in terms of the causal history of words themselves. Saul Kripke (1940–), Gareth Evans (1946–1980), and Hilary Putnam (1926–) have all defended versions of this theory. As we have seen, a descriptivist theory of reference does not imply that naming words and phrases necessarily correspond to objects in the world. Causal theorists, on the other hand, insist that naming words and phrases originate with an initial act of naming, or *linguistic baptism*, as Kripke calls it, and that those words then spread out through communities of language users. My use of the term "Plato," for example, means that I am connected to Plato in a causal chain that extends back to the naming of a certain child in ancient Greece who went on to write many famous works of philosophy. Obviously, I am not causally connected to an actual object when I use the term "the tooth fairy," but I am linked via causal chains to whoever first coined the expression "tooth fairy," who in turn was connected to the originators of the words "tooth" and "fairy," and so on.

Theories of meaning and reference are just the tip of the iceberg when it comes to the philosophical issues revolving around how the world, our minds and language are related. Another such issue concerns the extent to which language constitutes reality itself. The formative role language plays in shaping and structuring our worldviews is extremely powerful. We get a glimpse of this whenever we notice a speaker of a language struggle because she cannot find a satisfactory way to translate some word, concept or idea into another language. Furthermore, sentences in languages such as English make extensive use of the subject-predicate form. As I suggested in the discussion of Aristotle in Chapter One, it is probably no coincidence that users of such languages tend to carve up the world in terms of objects and their properties, since subject terms are typically objects and predicates are typically properties.

A question that arises at this point is whether our entire conscious experience of the world is a function of language. In other words, is language the means with which we construct reality? The so-called Sapir-Whorf hypothesis, according to which language strongly determines the nature of human thought, evoked serious interest in this question several decades ago. Benjamin Whorf, a prominent American linguist, studied indigenous American languages and ventured the view that the tense structure of such languages actually determines how speakers of these languages experience time. Strong versions of the theory that language structures reality have fallen into disfavor in recent decades, however, as philosophers and linguists have taken the view that commonalities in the thought of speakers of different languages far outweigh differences arising from linguistic diversity. Moreover, elegant experiments in psychology have shown that human subjects are capable of performing complex cognitive feats, such as mentally rotating shapes, which appear to be language-independent. Translating between languages is fraught with nuances and difficulties. Indeed, as we saw in the introductory chapter, W.V. Quine takes translation between languages to be so obscure as to be essentially indeterminate; but it does not necessarily follow from this that speakers of different languages are therefore so isolated from each other that they inhabit literally different worlds.

Language use pervades every human culture. Noam Chomsky (1928–) has developed a highly influential theory of linguistics to explain this phenomenon and several other features of language acquisition and use. Chomsky argues that, as diverse as they are, all natural languages spring from an innate, biologically endowed language facility that we all share as humans. Not only is this abstract facility, called a universal grammar, responsible for generating every natural language, Chomsky thinks that it also helps us understand how and why children are so adept at language acquisition. His theory makes for interesting comparisons with evolutionary accounts of psychology, and also with Immanuel Kant's earlier and more general idea that we structure and interpret the world in accordance with innate cognitive faculties, of which more in the next chapter. Chomsky's influence as both a linguist and a left-wing critic of the US government policies is far-reaching. The ramifications of his theories on contemporary philosophy of mind are exemplified in the work of Jerry Fodor (1935–), who takes thought to be represented in language-like terms, a thesis that goes by the name of the *language of thought*.

This brings to an end our brief survey of issues in the philosophy of language. It is important to bear in mind that we have restricted ourselves exclusively to problems in the analytic tradition of the philosophy of language. We have disregarded altogether an alternative movement in the philosophy of language that traces back to the Swiss linguist Ferdinand de Saussure (1857–1913) and culminates in a general theory of signs called *semiotics*. This movement continues to exert considerable influence, particularly in Europe. Questions about the scope and limits of language are by no means isolated from other areas of philosophical inquiry, however, and reappear throughout the remainder of this chapter and the next.

2.2: LOGIC, REASONING, AND ARGUMENTATION

In addition to language, our faculty of reason is an indispensable tool in philosophy and everyday life, and understanding the nature of it is also vital if we are to develop our acumen as philosophers. Logic is the study of reasoning and argumentation, and in this section we explore some aspects of its history and nature.

Reasoning comes into play in virtually every complex problem-solving and decision-making process we undertake, and it arises whenever we attempt to conclude, or infer, some idea or statement on the basis of prior observations or assumptions. We conclude that four is less than six if five is less than six and four is less than five; we infer that it is cold outside if we look out the window and see icicles forming on the eaves; we deduce that a dead battery is not the reason that a car won't start because we observe that the battery is still charged; and so on. Chains of reasoning that culminate in an inference of some sort are called *arguments*. The word "argument" has several senses, and while it more commonly evokes the idea of an interpersonal conflict or disagreement, in logic it refers to a set of sentences, one of which is a conclusion and one or more of which are premises. (Technically, this definition of "argument" is not entirely right, but it is adequate for our purposes.) The premises of an argument are meant to lend support or give us reasons for accepting the conclusion, which may or may not follow from the premises with certainty.

There are at least two kinds of arguments, of which the most important are *deductive* and *inductive* arguments. A deductively valid argument is one in which the conclusion follows from the premise or premises with absolute logical certainty. Deductive arguments were studied extensively by Aristotle, who was the first major logician and perhaps still the greatest logician of all time. Here is an example of a deductive argument: *Calgary is in Alberta.*

Alberta is in Canada. Canada is in North America. Therefore Calgary is in North America. Here is another example: *All Martians are purple. Britney Spears is a Martian. Therefore Britney Spears is purple.* You will note from these examples that deductive arguments do not require the sentences comprising them to be true. Whether or not individual sentences are true or false does not determine whether an argument is valid. Rather, what makes an argument valid is that the conclusion follows from the premise or premises as a matter of logical certainty. In other words, an argument is valid if we are forced to accept that the conclusion follows from the premises in question, regardless of whether the premises or conclusion is actually true. Deductive reasoning is used extensively in mathematics, logic, and computer programming, as well as in some problem-solving activities. If we narrow down the causes of a car breakdown to either an alternator or a starter motor problem and then eliminate the alternator as a possible cause, we deduce that the problem lies with the starter motor. The clever deductions of Sherlock Holmes typically incorporate elements of deductive reasoning, but he also tends to rely on intelligent guesswork and inductive reasoning.

Inductive arguments are ones in which the premises give us only probable grounds for accepting the conclusion. If we learn that Pedro is an American and that 99 per cent of Americans have heard of Michael Jordan, then we are likely to conclude that Pedro has heard of Michael Jordan, even though we cannot be absolutely certain that this conclusion is correct. Similarly, if I were considering buying an Acme computer, but then read a series of negative consumer reports about Acme computers, I would likely pass on buying one, even though I could buy one that would function perfectly. But if inductive reasoning is never totally reliable, why do we resort to it at all? The reason is that, for better or worse, we are forced to rely on induction for much of our decision making because we find ourselves faced with drawing conclusions on the basis of incomplete information and a less than entirely predictable world.

Problems of induction have long afflicted both philosophers of science and the rest of us. We are all familiar with those ambushes that life springs upon us from time to time which force us to discard our expectations or assumptions. We discover with dismay and surprise, for instance, that we are out of milk; we are hapless victims of lightning strikes; we are the unsuspecting beneficiaries of windfalls or acts of kindness. In short, life teaches us to expect the unexpected. In the philosophy of science, induction turns out to form the basis of even the most firmly established of scientific laws, which are, according to Hume at least, mere inductive generalizations. We observe apples falling to the ground; we perform experiments with objects in controlled environments to study their motion; and we track the motion of heavenly bodies. On the basis of our detailed observation of these phenomena, we frame hypotheses and scientific laws to account for the phenomena. An example of one such law is Newton's inverse square law of gravitation. But while we expect the world to continue to conform to the laws of science in the future, the history of science is one vast graveyard of theories that were serviceable for a time before being scrapped or modified because they were not up to the task of dealing with new phenomena or observations.

We are driven to form generalizations on the basis of the behaviors and patterns that replicate themselves in nature and in the laboratory. But problems of induction associated with this process extend beyond the realms of philosophy of science and into the area of language as well. Nelson Goodman (1906–1998) has pointed out that the notion of what it is that observations actually confirm can be quite ambiguous. We take buttercups to be yellow because every buttercup we have observed to date happens to be yellow. But suppose we define a new predicate, *blellow*, to mean the colour that objects are if they are observed to be yellow on or before January 1st, 2020, and *blue* if they are not observed for the first time until *after* that date. This new predicate makes buttercups confirming instances of things that are both yellow *and* blellow. That is, buttercups are just as much blellow as they are yellow! The concept of blellow might seem silly at first, but the point is that it is no less silly than yellow. So-called paradoxes of induction such as this might seem to be irrelevant to everyday life, but the traps that await us when we become too complacent in our inductive reasoning show that those paradoxes actually have powerful lessons to teach us. Black swans would have struck Europeans as no less absurd than blue buttercups until black swans were discovered in Western Australia. And Bertrand Russell made an amusing point about the perils of induction with his story of the chicken that came to believe the farmer would always come to feed it on the basis of the chicken's experiences every morning. The chicken's naïve faith in induction was adequate until the day the farmer had chicken for dinner. End of story.

The study of logic really came into its own in the twentieth century, due in part because of the work of logicians and mathematicians including George Boole (1815–64), Frege, John von Neumann (1903–57), and Alan Turing, which paved the way for the then newly emerging field of computer science. Logic actually underpins both hardware and software in computer science: hardware because the switches and circuits through which electrical currents in computers flow are "logic gates," and software because programming languages rely on logical operations such as negation, conjunction and disjunction to encode the instructions that computers in turn execute. But while the study of logic reached maturity in the twentieth century, it by no means began then. Aristotle laid the foundations for logic with his exhaustive analysis of specialized deductive arguments known as *syllogisms*, of which the above argument about Britney Spears is an example. Medieval philosophers were also heavily engaged with problems of logic and theology, but important breakthroughs had to wait until the work of Frege, who devised a way of dealing with quantification in logic, which finally enabled logicians to better understand statements employing words such as "all," "some" and "no." The most important contribution to logic in the twentieth century came from Kurt Gödel, an Austrian-born, American logician. Unfortunately, Gödel's results are too technical to fully appreciate unless one has studied logic extensively, but they are so profound that it is worth mentioning that he proved what is called the completeness of first-order (or quantificational) logic, as well as the incompleteness of first-order logic when it is extended to include arithmetic. (A technical aside: a system of logic is said to be complete if it generates all of the truths that the system in question is capable of expressing.) We will have more to say about some potential implications of this striking result in the final chapter.

As interesting and practical as the pursuit of logic is in its own right, it is also an integral part of philosophy and crucially important for understanding philosophy as a whole. Formal systems of logic consist of two parts: syntactic and semantic components. Syntax defines the rules for constructing well formed expressions. Semantics deals with technical definitions of notions such as truth, validity, and the interpretation of certain symbols. But concepts such as truth and interpretation extend well beyond these systems and into other domains of philosophy, including metaphysics, epistemology, and the philosophy of language. Statements in logic are similar to sentences or statements in natural languages, although many logicians insist that statements in logic—or *propositions*, as they are also known—are abstract entities and not particular sentences of natural languages. To illustrate this point, observe that the three sentences *It's raining*, *Il pleut* and *Es regnet* are superficially quite different due to the fact that they belong to different languages, but to some logicians at least, they express one and the same underlying thought, or proposition.

Moreover, adopting certain laws of logic, such as the *law of excluded middle*, the *principle of bivalence* and the *principle of non-contradiction*, has potential implications for metaphysics as well. The law of excluded middle states that for any statement P, "P or not-P" is true. The closely related principle of bivalence asserts that for any statement P, either P is true or not-P is true. And the principle of non-contradiction states that for any statement P, it is not the case that both P is true and not-P is true. Now to the extent that a system of logic mirrors the world itself, the two-valued (or bivalent) logic we have adopted so far, which is also called classical logic, implies that every state of affairs in the world is determinately one way or not that way, with no middle ground. In other words, either it's snowing or it's not snowing, either one plus one equals two or one plus one does not equal two, and so on. The influential English philosopher Michael Dummett (1925–) rejects the principle of bivalence (though not the law of excluded middle), arguing that unless we have grounds for justifiably asserting that a statement or its negation is true, no objective fact of the matter attaches to what such statements assert. An example of a statement that Dummett would argue presents problems of verification is this: *The total number of brontosauruses that roamed the earth is 15,349,782.*

Accepting the principle of bivalence means, for example, denying that there is any vagueness or fuzziness in the world. Our use of language, linguistic descriptions, and the meanings of words may be vague or fuzzy, but this fuzziness doesn't necessarily extend to the world itself. On the other hand, if one takes the view that vagueness is indeed the way of the world, then our logic must reflect this, and so we should arguably relax some of the impossibly rigid laws of classical logic. Calls for this course of action have come from, among others, some philosophers of quantum physics, who argue that classical, bivalent logic cannot cope with the indeterminacy in the world they say quantum physics reveals.

2.3: Theories of Truth

"What is truth?", Pontius Pilate asked Jesus according to the Bible, and the answer still eludes us, although philosophers have hardly been at a loss for things to say about the topic. As we noted above, questions about the nature of truth lie at the intersection of logic, metaphysics, epistemology, and the philosophy of language. In this section, we survey some prominent theories of truth, after which I advance some views and arguments of my own.

One of the most enduring and influential theories of truth is the *correspondence theory* of truth. The idea here is that sentences in a language—more precisely indicative or declarative sentences— are true to the extent that they correspond to actual states of affairs. So, for example, the sentence "Calgary is in Alberta" is true if indeed there is a place in Alberta called Calgary. Likewise, "Whales swim" is true if whales really do swim, whereas "Calgary is in the Atlantic Ocean" is not true if there is no such place as Calgary in the Atlantic Ocean. This seems straightforward enough, but the theory embodies some controversial assumptions. First and foremost, the correspondence theory is predicated on the assumption that there are determinate states of affairs in the world, states of affairs, moreover, that we can accurately describe using language. Truth, according to this theory, consists in a certain relationship—the relationship of *correspondence*—that holds between some sentences and the world but not between all sentences and the world. True sentences supposedly exemplify this relationship, while false sentences do not.

But what exactly is this relationship of correspondence? True sentences do not mirror reality in any literal way. After all, the sentence "snow is white" is neither snowy nor white. Nor are true sentences models of reality in the way that, say, a toy Ford Mustang models a real Ford Mustang. So what exactly does the relation of correspondence consist in? If we could somehow get outside our heads and compare the statements we make about the world with the world as it really is, then presumably we could determine whether our statements do indeed correspond to the world. But since this is not an option, explicating the precise nature of correspondence remains a key weakness of this theory, notwithstanding its initial air of plausibility.

Most of the competitors of the correspondence theory of truth tend to downplay metaphysical concepts such as correspondence and the objectivity of reality, and urge instead that truth is a function of either knowledge or language. A theory that combines both of these aspects is the *coherence theory*, articulated most definitively by Brand Blanshard (1892–1987). According to this account of truth, we develop in the course of our experience bodies of beliefs and knowledge on both an individual and social level. Moreover, we seek to unify our knowledge in a cohesive fashion. Coherence theorists take the truth of a particular statement to be a function of how well that statement coheres with one's overall experience. We accept as true those beliefs that fit in with our overall systems of belief and reject as false those that don't. The coherence theory takes the interconnectedness and overall cohesion of our knowledge to be the standard against which we judge statements to be true or false. But although we undeniably place a premium on overall coherence as a desideratum when it comes to our body of knowledge, it is questionable whether this alone counts, or even ought to count, as the measure of truth. To appreciate this problem, we need only reflect on the fact that competing ways in which people structure their overall worldviews, including those based on astrology, science, various religious outlooks and even conspiracy theories can be at the same time internally coherent and yet mutually incompatible. If this is the case, then the notion of truth becomes relativized to each of those different worldviews, thereby losing much of its philosophical interest and significance.

A somewhat similar theory to the coherence theory but one that focuses more heavily on the utility of truth is the *pragmatic* theory of truth. This theory was developed and refined by several American philosophers around the turn of the twentieth century, most notably Charles Sanders Peirce (1839–1914), John Dewey (1859–1952), and William James (1842–1910), and it has continued to exert a strong influence on such recent American philosophers as Quine, Putnam, and Richard Rorty (1931–). The early pragmatists tended to maintain a keen interest in the sciences, and they took a practical approach to truth as consisting in satisfactory answers to our problems or questions, especially scientific questions. Truth for pragmatists, then, is a matter of what works best when it comes to searching for answers to our theoretical investigations. Some scientifically inclined pragmatists appeal to criteria such as corroboration and verification as providing benchmarks for the truth of beliefs, but in general it is usefulness, or "whatever works," that is the final arbiter of truth for pragmatists. This theory, however, is subject to the same kinds of objections to which the coherence theory is vulnerable. For example, one person might find it useful to maintain the belief that God exists, but if someone else has no use whatsoever for this belief, what are we to say about the claim that God exists? Of course, God's existence is not necessarily something we can verify, but if we take utility to be the ultimate criterion of truth, then verification is beside the point anyway. We appear to be forced to conclude that belief in God is true for the believer and not true for the non-believer, but this is hardly a satisfactory conclusion for anyone who thinks that truth must come down to more than a matter of one person's word against another's.

Suppose, on the other hand, that we simply accept the view that truth is nothing more than one person's word against another's. This would mean that what might be true for one person—let's say the belief that one plus one equals two—might be false for someone else. The theory that truth is entirely subjective is known as *relativism*. Relativism is perennially attractive as a way of thinking about truth for a number of reasons. First, as we have noted in our critique of the correspondence theory, the notion that there is an objective world out there which true statements accurately describe is exceedingly difficult to establish. And secondly, as we become increasingly sensitive to, and tolerant of, the fact that people from different cultures appear to have diverse worldviews, the claim that there is a single, objective reality has come to be regarded by many as dogmatic, outdated, and even as symptomatic of intolerance towards different worldviews.

Is relativism viable as a theory of truth? The answer to this depends very much on whether one demands consistency of a theory of truth. A thoroughgoing relativist has to accept, for example, that *Two plus two equals four* may be true for one person but not necessarily true for someone else. But to conclude from this relativity of beliefs that two plus two does *and* does not equal four is an outright contradiction. Short of simply accepting contradictions, the only defense left open to the relativist is to assert that two plus two equals four is true relative to person X, but not true relative to person Y. But regardless of whether relativists can elude contradictions, or even care to elude contradictions, another problem is that relativism is self-refuting. What does a relativist say about the truth of relativism itself? That is, what is her answer to the question *Is relativism true?* If she is sincere in her relativism, she will have to concede that the theory is true only for herself and her fellow relativists, and so non-relativists can disregard the theory in safety. On the other hand, to answer that relativism is absolutely true is to refute the very theory the relativist espouses.

The question, then, is whether the relativist's willingness to accommodate contradictions or self-refutation leaves her with a worthwhile conception of truth at all. On the other hand, a decisive refutation of relativism seems to be unavailable to the non-relativist, as the relativist is always able to rebut any assertion X that the non-relativist might advance by insisting, "But X is true only for *you*." In other words, someone with a robust sense of truth can engage a relativist only to the extent that the relativist shares this robust sense of truth; since the relativist doesn't, then debating a relativist is futile. Although relativism may well be irrefutable, that is not a good enough reason to accept it; and perhaps the best way to confront relativists is to ask them whether they indeed tolerate apparent contradictions on a routine basis in their day-to-day lives. It is at this point that most self-styled relativists run into difficulty, as accepting contradictions habitually makes for an extremely odd and impractical *modus vivendi*. We shall have more to say about these issues when we discuss relativism in the context of ethics in Chapter Four.

The semantic theory of truth, first articulated by the Polish-born American logician Alfred Tarski (1902–83), attracted widespread attention in the latter part of the twentieth century. Tarski's most important work was in formal languages and in how to define truth in such languages, but his work was motivated in part by problems associated with the notion of truth in natural languages. Now we use languages to express propositions, propositions that we deem to be true or false, but any natural language with the resources to express the predicate "is true" is notoriously capable of generating paradoxes such as the famous Liar Paradox. Suppose that liars are by definition people who utter nothing but lies, and that an Australian proclaims, "All Australians are liars." Non-Australians can assert that all Australians are liars without generating a paradox, but what about Australians? If an Australian states that all Australians are liars, then the statement "All Australians are liars," if it is true, must be a lie; but if what the Australian proclaims is false, it is a lie, in which case it confirms the truth of the statement that all Australians are liars. This is the Liar Paradox. Tarski circumvented this problem in the case of formal languages by deferring semantic concepts such as "is true" to a metalanguage in which we can speak about and interpret sentences in the original object language.

The example Tarski originally used to illustrate this point is this:

The sentence "snow is white" is true, if, and only if, snow is white.

In general, a sentence x is true if and only if p, where p represents a sentence we refer to as true and x designates p. For Tarski, a definition of truth is adequate insofar as it generates all equivalences of the above form, and truth itself is the relation that holds between a state of affairs, such as snow is white, and a sentence that *satisfies* the state of affairs in question, which in this case is the whiteness of snow. This maneuver allows us to reformulate the issue of the truth of "All Australians are liars" as follows:

The sentence "All Australians are liars" is true if and only if all Australians are liars,

where the original claim made by the Australian liar is now embedded within a larger sentence of what logicians call a metalanguage.

Actually, Tarski's technique succeeds in dispelling liar-type paradoxes most definitively in formal languages, where the crucial distinction between so-called object languages and metalanguages is effectively specifiable. In a natural language such as English, the distinction between levels of languages remains internal to English.

In some respects, the semantic theory bears a close resemblance to the correspondence theory, and in fact some philosophers have claimed that it amounts to a sophisticated restatement of the correspondence theory. But it is important to keep in mind that correspondence theorists insist that sentences refer to a reality beyond language, whereas the semantic theory makes no such metaphysical commitment. The satisfaction relation Tarski uses to define the truth predicate is a semantic (and thus linguistic) notion, albeit a notion belonging to a metalanguage. On the other hand, some correspondence theorists see the semantic theory as complementing their own theory, pending further explanation of the satisfaction relation.

The overtly technical and linguistic direction of modern theories of truth have left some philosophers unimpressed, because while they concede that we use language to express truths, they do not agree that it follows that truth itself is semantic or linguistic in nature. "Truth" and "is true" are words, to be sure, but to regard truth as a purely linguistic or semantic notion fails, for example, to explain why truth matters to us. Why should we care whether anyone speaks truly or falsely? Tarski's theory is silent on this point. Tarski deals with how truth functions as a predicate within a hierarchy of formal languages; but the relevance of his account to the nature of truth beyond formal systems is moot. On the other hand, the technique of invoking a hierarchy of languages—also called semantic ascent—deftly handles the problem of truth and self-reference generated by liar-type sentences.

There are, however, alternatives to the approaches to truth we have surveyed so far. One interesting theory that receives scant attention these days is Frege's account of truth. Frege thought that sentences as a whole are names, and that they name one of two truth-values: the True and the False. According to Frege, in a language that is formulated rigorously enough, each of its sentences will be true or false and will thus name the True and the False accordingly. Nowadays his theory is seen as metaphysically profligate and quaint, but while postulating the peculiar entities the True and the False was certainly an odd move, Frege was, in my view, quite right to imply that truth is essentially metaphysical in nature. Indeed, I would argue that anyone who thinks that truth extends further than language and the human mind ought to acknowledge this.

On the view I am urging, the truth is very much out there. We have no choice but to use language to express and communicate specific truths, and to express our understanding of the concept via words such as "truth"; but it does not follow from this that truth itself is purely linguistic or mind-dependent. To construe truth in this explicitly metaphysical way presupposes that there is a reality outside of us in which truth actually resides. The conception of truth I am sketching, which we can call the *ontological*, or *objective*, conception of truth, stands or falls with this presupposition. The essential difference between this conception of truth and the correspondence theory is that, unlike the correspondence theory, it denies that truth consists in a relationship of some sort. That is, it does not construe truth as a correspondence relation between statements and relevant states of affairs in the world. Rather, the claim is that truth is itself ontological in nature; truth is identified directly with the objective and external reality that it presupposes exists. The correspondence theory also makes this presupposition and takes ontology seriously, but the ontological conception of truth does not assume that language is up to the task of expressing truth.

Where does this get us? In terms of helping us discriminate between true and false statements, this conception of truth gets us absolutely nowhere. I must stress that we are not talking about a theory of truth in the ordinary sense of the term, but rather something weaker than that: a mere *conception* of what truth is. Can we "get at" an external, extra-linguistic reality? Alas, no. For reasons that will become more evident in the next chapter, in our discussion of the British empiricists and Kant, there is unfortunately no way we can get outside our heads and apprehend external reality directly. This does not mean that no such world exists, although it does mean that there is exceedingly little we can say about it with any confidence. To concede that we can say virtually nothing about this world beyond our ken admittedly renders one's commitment to it little more than an act of faith, but philosophers from Plato to Gödel have been prepared to take this step, although some philosophers, such as Plato, make vague appeals to faculties of insight or intuition that supposedly allow us to access external reality. Whatever the status of such accounts, if declaring our faith in the existence of an inaccessible, external reality is ultimately the best, or the only, way to make sense of the world as we experience it, then in my view this is a step we are compelled to take.

We endeavor to express truth via language, but if the truth we attempt to express is strictly speaking inaccessible to us, then the "truths" we express are, at best, educated guesses. So the conception of truth I am defending does not take us far at all when it comes to understanding truth strictly in terms of the linguistic predicate "is true." However, my pessimism about our prospects for acquiring or expressing truths in language is quite separate from my *commitment* to truth as an objective concept, which I am urging is how the notion of truth is best understood.

One virtue of the metaphysical conception of truth is that, as opposed to rival theories, it explains why truth is a matter of vital importance to us. Other theories attempt to spell out what it is for a sentence in a language to be true, but they are neutral with respect to whether it is important that we utter truths rather than falsehoods, or indeed whether truth matters at all. If you tell a child who is depending on your help to cross a highway: "It's safe to cross now," much depends on whether your assessment of the highway traffic is right. What you tell the child is a matter of life and death, and for the sake of the child you want to get it right!

Of course, whether we should place more value on children being alive than dead is a moral question, but my point is that striving to attain truth is a matter of striving to "get it right" when it comes to what the world is really like, and that our efforts in this connection are also profoundly moral in nature. Language represents our best effort as humans to build a reliable bridge to the outside world, but there is no guarantee that the bridge rests on secure foundations. As C.B. Martin likes to put it, we have to be lucky!

It is important not to lose sight of the different issues and questions surrounding truth. Questions about how we acquire truth, that is, questions about our knowledge of truth, are distinct from questions about how the words like "true" and "truth" function in language, which are semantic issues. And then there is the position I am urging, which is that truth, appearances notwithstanding, is properly understood as a metaphysical concept. I revisit this metaphysical conception of truth towards the end of the book, where I argue that commitment to an ontological conception of truth amounts to a commitment to *metaphysical realism*, and that the two stand or fall together. In the next and final section, we discuss some distinctions concerning true statements that have long exercised philosophers, most notably Kant and Kripke.

2.4: KANT AND KRIPKE ON ANALYTIC, SYNTHETIC, NECESSARY, AND CONTINGENT TRUTHS

So far we have talked about the truth of statements as if truths are entirely undifferentiated. But some philosophers have argued that not all truth statements are of the same kind. In particular, they have argued that there are important distinctions to be made between analytic and synthetic truths, and between necessary and contingent truths.

Immanuel Kant urged that we classify declarative statements, or judgments as he called them, as either *analytic* or *synthetic*. Analytic statements are those in which the meaning of the predicate is contained within the subject. For example, the statement

"All bachelors are unmarried men" is analytic, according to Kant, because to be a bachelor just *is* to be an unmarried man. On the other hand, "The sky is blue" is synthetic, because the meaning of the word "blue" is not contained in "sky." But what about this example: "All English teachers are English"? Is it analytic or synthetic? The answer is that on one interpretation it is analytic and on another it is synthetic. That is, "All teachers *from* England are English" is analytic, while "All teachers *of* English are English" is synthetic.

Assuming that all subject-predicate statements really do fall into one of these two categories, we might ask if there are any aspects of the world or human knowledge that this distinction reflects. One possibility—but I must stress that it is only a possibility—is that it is based on the distinction between so-called *a priori* and *a posteriori* knowledge. *A priori* means "prior to experience," and so *a priori* knowledge is knowledge we possess prior to, or independent of, our experience. Apart from strict tautologies such as *Twenty is twenty*, arguments on behalf of *a priori* knowledge are notoriously controversial. The theorems of logic and mathematics appear to be relatively safe as candidates for *a priori* knowledge because they seem to rely so little on experience. By contrast, *a posteriori* knowledge is knowledge we acquire in the course of experience. We learn that birds have feathers; that the sky is blue; that dinosaurs no longer roam the earth, and so on. Clearly, truths such as these are not matters of reason alone; rather, we find them to be true via experience.

The epistemological concepts of *a priori* and *a posteriori* knowledge closely parallel the metaphysical concepts of *necessary* and *contingent* truths. Necessary truths—for example: "Either it's raining or it's not raining"—are ones that cannot possibly be false, whereas contingent truths are truths that happen to be true, but as a matter of logic could just as easily be false. "Hitler became Chancellor of Germany in 1933" happens to be true, unfortunately, but a unique set of historical circumstances helped shape his political destiny, and were it not for those circumstances he could easily have remained a second-rate Austrian artist. This, then, is an example of a contingent truth. The distinction between necessary and contingent truths has generated an entire branch of logic called *modal logic*, which has been abetted by, among others, Leibniz, C.I. Lewis (1883–1964), Kripke, and David Lewis. Some logicians, most famously Leibniz and David Lewis, interpret the difference between necessary and contingent truths in terms of the concept of possible worlds. That is, necessary truths are supposedly true in all possible worlds—or *at* all possible worlds as possible worlds theorists put it—whereas contingent truths are supposed to be true at some worlds and false at others. Thus, the logical possibility that Hitler never rose to power in Germany is construed as meaning that there are possible worlds in which Hitler never rose to power in Germany. Necessary falsehoods, such as "square circles exist," are said to be false in all possible worlds.

W.V. Quine and other philosophers have attacked Kant's hard and fast analytic-synthetic distinction. Quine argued forcefully that our knowledge is holistic in nature. According to Quine, our knowledge is made up of a web of beliefs, and while some of these beliefs, such as theorems of mathematics and logic, are more firmly embedded in this web than others, he insisted that in principle none of our beliefs is immune from revision. But in an even more startling challenge to orthodox thinking in this area, Kripke refuted the traditional association of necessary truths with *a priori* knowledge on the one hand and contingent truth with *a posteriori* knowledge on the other. In particular, he argued that some necessary truths are *a posteriori* and that some contingent truths are *a priori*. As an example of the former, he cites the fact that chemically speaking, water is H_2O. This is necessarily true, but its truth was discovered only in the course of empirical research and so is known to us only *a posteriori*. And as an example of the latter, he cites the standard meter bar, a platinum bar in Paris that defines the length of a meter. That *that* particular bar is one meter long is contingent, in the sense that we could have chosen another bar to define the length of a meter, but it is also *a priori*, since we assign the length one meter to that particular bar—we do not learn that the bar is one meter long through experience. Kripke's fascinating work continues to stimulate debate in the fields of philosophical logic and metaphysics.

CHAPTER 3

Epistemology:
Knowledge and Doubt

Where is the wisdom we have lost in knowledge?
Where is the knowledge we have lost in information?

— T.S. Eliot

There are knowns, known unknowns and unknown unknowns.

— Popular saying

3.0: Introduction

If you wanted to make a detailed list of everything you know, what would be on your list? You might begin with information about your name, address, date of birth, the names of various family members and friends, and so on. You might add to this list descriptions of what you had for your last meal, the clothes you are currently wearing or were last wearing, assorted facts about your employment history, and the country you live in. Your list might also take in miscellaneous entries about places you have visited or even places you have heard about but never actually seen. Maybe you happen to know that Quito is the capital of

69

Ecuador, or that electrons orbit the nuclei of atoms. We acquire these and myriad other facts from books, television programs, teachers, and so on. The list goes on and on. Before long, you would likely abandon the project were you to realize just how tedious this task would be.

But even if you managed to list all of the facts you know, what about other forms of knowledge? You presumably also know all sorts of other things, such as how to ride a bicycle, how to create a good impression with your parents and how to play several games. Perhaps you know how to bake delicious muffins or how to comfort your best friend when she is feeling sad. How, if at all, does our skills-based, or "how to" knowledge relate to our list of the things we know? Then there is the introspective self-knowledge we possess. It seems that we all have privileged and intimate knowledge about ourselves and of what it feels like for each of us to be ourselves. We do not, and perhaps cannot, ever expect others to have this knowledge, although of course we sometimes also delude ourselves in ways that are recognizable to others but not to ourselves. What are we to make of self-knowledge and the possibility that in some respects we might not know our true selves even if we think we do? As the old saying goes, it ain't what you know that's the problem, but what you "know" that ain't so. For practical as well as philosophical purposes, what we don't know can be no less significant than what we do know. While we may know *that* we do not know certain things, by definition we do not know precisely *what* those things are. For example, I do know that I don't know Madonna's phone number; what I don't know, of course, is what that number actually is.

Some things we know, or at least *claim* to know, first-hand through direct experience. Your awareness that you are currently reading a book, for example, comes to you directly, right now, via your experience. Other things we do not know in this way, but rather recall or believe because the knowledge comes from what we take to be reliable sources. Nevertheless, we are very often confident that we know many things of this sort. If, like me, you have no first-hand experience of the planet Pluto, your liver, or sub-atomic particles, does this mean you are less confident that you know such things than you are about the items on the first shopping list you ever wrote? If you are at all like me, you probably remember nothing about the first shopping list you ever wrote. We frequently defer to experts, teachers, the media, books, friends and acquaintances for much of what we think of as the knowledge we possess, even though we soon come to realize that doing so leaves us susceptible to misinformation, distortions, and deceptions, especially if we rely indiscriminately on such knowledge.

On the other hand, some of our knowledge seems to have nothing to do with experience at all, either directly or indirectly. For example, we may be certain, or at any rate be as certain as we are of anything, that if all Canadians pay taxes and Amandeep is a Canadian, then Amandeep pays taxes. Our certainty that Amandeep pays taxes, as we saw in the previous chapter, has nothing to do with whether or not we happen to know Amandeep personally, or know of Amandeep, or even whether Amandeep actually exists. Rather, our certainty consists in the fact that the statement "Amandeep pays taxes" follows logically from assuming, at least provisionally, that all Canadians pay taxes and that Amandeep is a Canadian. What our certainty pertains to, that is to say, is a particular *inference*. In a similar vein, I know that 402 plus 296 equals 698, even though I have never actually counted out exactly 402 items and added them to 296 other items to confirm that this comes to 698 items. What are we to make of the origins and status of these more abstract knowledge claims, which apparently lie outside of experience altogether but nevertheless seem to exemplify a form of timeless and indubitable knowledge?

Aside from a few wise people—Socrates and the late physicist Richard Feynman come to mind—who insouciantly claim to know nothing, most of us routinely lay claim to knowing many things. But what is the basis of our knowledge claims, and how certain can we be that we know what we profess to know? After all, we have all felt the keen disappointment of discovering that our confidence about some of our "knowledge" was totally misplaced. Anyone who has unexpectedly flunked an exam or quiz is all too familiar with this experience. Our embarrassment is that much more acute if we realize that we have misled others in our ignorance. How do we go about determining what we do and do not know for sure and, given our all too human propensity for error, is there anything we can really know for sure? If we are mistaken about some things some of the time, might we be mistaken about what we know—or at least what we think we know—all the time? Can it make sense for us to doubt *everything* we think we know, or do we reach a point where systematically doubting what we know eventually defeats itself? Are there different *forms* of knowledge, or indeed different ways of knowing? What is the relationship between knowledge and belief? Can knowledge be explained in evolutionary terms, just as we explain our genetic heritage? And how does knowledge relate to information? These and related questions form the central concerns of this chapter. But before we can hope to construct a positive account of knowledge, we must first confront the challenge posed by the galling fact that each of us finds that we are sometimes wrong about what we think we know.

3.1: Nagging Doubts: The Challenge of Skepticism

We all entertain doubts from time to time about various claims before us, which for the most part is just as well. The proverbial offer of some prime real estate in Florida is meant to remind us not to be too gullible about accepting a deal that seems too good to be true. Healthy skepticism is just that, but does it follow that to be extremely skeptical is extremely healthy? This section is about the answer to that question and more generally about the nature of philosophical skepticism.

We can entertain doubts of one sort or another about virtually any knowledge claim, and casting doubts upon knowledge claims in general is, in itself, unremarkable. Philosophical skepticism, however, consists in systematically doubting our pretensions to knowledge. Skepticism has occupied a venerable place in the history of Western philosophy, dating back to the Pre-Socratics. Perhaps the most direct and dramatic of all challenges to the possibility of knowledge came from Gorgias of Leontini (*c.* 480 B.C.E.), who bluntly asserted that human knowledge is impossible. Sextus Empiricus (third century B.C.E.) reported in *Adversus Mathematicos* VII 65 that in a lost work entitled *On Nature or the Non-Existent,* Gorgias claimed: "Nothing exists; if anything does exist it is unknowable; and granting it even to exist and to be knowable by any one man, it could never be communicated to others." Whatever arguments Gorgias may have mustered in defense of this audacious and nihilistic position have long since disappeared. In the absence of supporting arguments, however, his position loses much of its force and interest, fascinating as it is.

An alternative strategy consists in challenging any knowledge claim x with the question "How do you know x?" This skeptic tends to challenge the adequacy of whatever the knower proposes as a basis for her knowledge claim, whether that response consists in deference to some authority, the supposed certainty of certain truths of reason or logic, or the knower's conviction in the incorrigibility of her first-hand experiences. Whichever strategy the knower defends, the skeptic is always free to retort: "But how does *this* guarantee certain knowledge?" Such dialogues tend to play themselves out until one or the other participant eventually gives up in frustration or simply changes the subject, with neither side having prevailed decisively.

Casting wholesale doubts upon our knowledge in the ways described above, however, invites the question as to what motivation we have for doing so. Perhaps the best rationale for taking philosophical skepticism seriously comes from René Descartes in his classic *Meditations,* published in 1641. These highly personal, almost confessional musings were undertaken over the course of several evenings, and they chronicle Descartes's search to spell out the foundations of absolutely certain knowledge. As a pre-eminent mathematician and scientist as well as philosopher, Descartes regarded it as imperative that he should achieve rigor in the foundations of human knowledge.

Descartes began by enquiring about the sources of his knowledge and noted that these sources typically consist of his senses. His knowledge of the world, that is to say, seemed to him to arise from his senses of sight, touch, hearing, and so on. So far, so good, but then he noted that sensory knowledge is notoriously unreliable, an observation confirmed by psychologists and neurophysiologists who study how our brains process and interpret sensory input. Examples abound of the ways in which our brains mislead us in the process of conjuring up the highly selective mental representations we mistake for faithful facsimiles of an external world. Such phenomena are discussed at length in psychology textbooks, but we will restrict ourselves to a brief discussion of some simple and familiar cases.

Consider how distant objects like trees look much smaller than nearby trees, the way in which straight railway tracks appear to converge and meet at a point on the horizon, or the way our eyes are fooled by good magicians. Tables and chairs appear to be solid, but physicists tell us they consist of atoms that in turn comprise mostly space between their subatomic constituents. Then there are the idiosyncratic ways in which our brains process ambiguous input, as in the examples of the Necker cube and the duck-rabbit figure cited in Chapter One. In these cases, we find that we alternate between different and mutually exclusive interpretations of one and the same image. In addition, brain performance can be altered or compromised by factors such as fatigue, unusual environmental conditions, stress, or mind-altering chemicals.

The point is that our cognitive faculties are susceptible to all kinds of internal and external influences and that this affects the way we process sensory stimuli in constructing representations of the world. Descartes realized that our reliance upon sensory experience as a source of certain knowledge raises a general problem. The difficulty is that if our senses indeed mislead us some of the time, is it possible that they do so on a routine basis? How can you be sure that your current sensory experiences accurately mirror reality? Can you be completely confident that at this very moment you are not undergoing an exceptionally vivid dream or even a hallucination? Might reading these words be part of a vast dream or drug-induced state resulting from powerful drugs someone slipped into your last meal? In the first *Meditation*, Descartes entertained the possibility that he is at the mercy of a hypothetical, all-powerful, evil demon who systematically deludes him about the reality of everything he experiences. What guarantee, he wondered, does he have that he is nothing but a hapless victim of such an entity?

A modern-day variation of Descartes's puzzle was proposed by the Harvard philosopher Hilary Putnam, who invites you to imagine that you are really a brain in a vat, kept alive in a laboratory by a scientist who inhabits a world beyond your experience, but who has recently succeeded in downloading the contents of vast computer programs into this brain. These programs are replete with memories of your past; a sense of personal identity which coincides with your own; experiences of an outside world, which happens to be the world you experience; and so on. Can you refute the possibility that you are really a brain in a vat? Philosophers have devised ever more sophisticated scenarios of this sort in their debates about the possibility of certain knowledge. These debates are far from resolved, but suffice it to say that Descartes took the prospect of this radical skepticism very seriously in his first *Meditation*.

What hope do we have of attaining a solid foundation for knowledge if we follow Descartes and concede that the existence of an evil demon is a real possibility? Descartes admitted to feeling deep despair about the implications of the Pandora's box of doubt he had opened until a way out of the dilemma dawned upon him. He reasoned that whatever doubts he might have had about the reliability of his sensory experience, he could be certain that while he was entertaining doubts, he was nevertheless still *thinking*. After all, to be experiencing doubts is to be thinking, and so regardless of the extent to which he might have worried that his doubts undermined his prospects for certain knowledge, he could ironically rest assured that the very fact that he was experiencing doubts confirmed to him that he was thinking! He thought he had finally found something that was beyond doubt, and this epiphany culminated in one of the most famous maxims in philosophy. Originally formulated as the Latin dictum *cogito ergo sum*, Descartes's immortal one-liner translates into English as *I think, therefore I am.* According to Descartes, the *cogito*, as it is commonly known, is a fundamental, indubitable truth, something that for Descartes cannot but be true whenever he is thinking. Having established to his own satisfaction that he had found an absolutely solid foundation for knowledge, Descartes endeavoured in the remainder of the *Meditations* to reconstruct a much more substantial body of knowledge. But what exactly does the *cogito* teach us?

The *cogito* has a highly experiential quality to it. Descartes might have satisfied himself that whenever he experienced thoughts he existed, but this is not a proof for anyone other than Descartes himself. The power and cogency of the *cogito* arises when we try it out for ourselves, so to speak. But this is problematic because however intuitive or obviously valid it might have seemed to Descartes—or to anyone who reflects upon it—the *cogito* is nevertheless highly subjective and context-sensitive. Unfortunately, this is considerably less than what we would expect from any objective, mind-independent truth. On the other hand, although both the premise and conclusion of the *cogito* emerge directly out of Descartes's subjective experiences, the *inference* between his thinking and his existing is a matter of reason, not experience; and in this sense the *cogito* is arguably objective after all. So, while Descartes uncovered deeply disturbing questions of skepticism in the course of investigating whether sensory experience can yield certain knowledge, over the course of the *Meditations* he managed to satisfy himself that there is a way out of the dead-end of skepticism, a process originating with the *cogito*.

David Hume arrived at skepticism by a different route but came to less optimistic conclusions about prospects for its resolution. Hume addressed basic questions about knowledge and metaphysics from an empiricist standpoint. He was especially interested in what we would now call philosophical psychology, specifically with how our minds process raw sensory input and generate abstract thoughts and ideas. We are all familiar with the phenomenon of cause and effect, but Hume offered a radical explanation of the relationship between our perceptions, or *impressions*, as he called them, and causes and effects. Hume argued that our preconceptions about causes and effects do not mirror the existence of real or necessary connections in the world, but merely reflect the recurring patterns and regularities that pervade our experience. We have a habit of assuming that causation is real, but for Hume causation consists simply in the association of some impressions with others. Our repeated and regular experience of seeing heavy objects fall when they are dropped, for example, leads us to infer that a causal relationship exists between an object above the ground being released and its falling to the ground. But, again, Hume interprets this relation-ship as strictly speaking associated with our impressions rather than as an inbuilt feature of the world. Hume consistently applied this same psychological approach to other areas of meta-physics as well, which would later stir Immanuel Kant from what he called his "metaphysical slumbers."

Hume's skepticism presents such a stern challenge to rational-ist preconceptions that reading him leaves one wondering whether pursuing metaphysics is an exercise in futility. Hume realized that his resolutely skeptical attitude toward metaphysics is ultimately a dead end, and he resigned himself to this conclu-sion. Following Hume's reasoning to its logical conclusion leaves us with a world in which there is just one event after another, none of which have any rhyme or reason other than whatever order we impose upon those events. And while some are sanguine about the impasse that this leaves us with, others reject Hume's skepticism as no less idle than the metaphysical speculation he sought so adamantly to banish. Hume cuts through nonsense and subjects speculative flights of fancy to harsh critical scrutiny, but while this is perfectly worthy, too much of a good thing in this case leaves us to question whether there is a compelling reason to abandon metaphysics after all. A Humean skeptic is never at risk of mistakenly accepting any faulty metaphysical theory, but is also disengaged from the vital involvement of so many of us in everyday life, and indeed in philosophy itself.

An alternative response to the radical skeptic is to argue that her position is self-defeating. The argument is that in order for the skeptic to deny the possibility of knowledge about x, she has first to acknowledge, at least implicitly, that we know x. For example, if a skeptic claims that she doesn't know whether she really has a body, the critic's rejoinder in this case would be that, even to formulate this skeptical claim, she has to betray her familiarity with the very thing she claims she cannot know she has for certain: her body. Another tack, due to G.E. Moore, is to defend common sense knowledge. Moore thought that certain states of affairs—for example the fact that he has two hands—are so self-evident that it simply makes no sense to doubt them. What these rejoinders to the radical skeptic share is a sense of the idleness of skepticism, and this point is well taken.

In the end, *radical* skepticism makes no practical difference to the way we live our lives, although more moderate forms of skepticism may make us, for example, more wary consumers. Admitting that our knowledge is fallible is surely not a compelling reason to give up on knowledge altogether. For all intents and purposes we conduct our lives as if we know with confidence that we are subject to the force of gravity, for example. And notwithstanding the fact that our knowledge claims are sometimes controverted and shown to be dead wrong, philosophies that do not do justice to the kinds of things that, for better or worse, we *claim* to know, tend to command neither widespread nor lasting support.

3.2: CAUSAL THEORIES OF KNOWLEDGE

Eschewing radical skepticism as a philosophical *cul-de-sac* and assuming that at least some of our knowledge is genuine, let us return to the question of the origins of our knowledge. As Descartes noted, much of our knowledge of the world seems to come to us via our senses. Humean doubts notwithstanding, this suggests that there is some sort of cause and effect relationship between events or objects in the world and the mental representations from which our knowledge of them springs. The empirical approach to the theory of knowledge John Locke articulated provides a suitable basis upon which to build a causal theory of knowledge.

We encountered something of Locke's general philosophical outlook in Chapter One, where we discussed his view that we inhabit a material world that impinges upon our senses, and that our senses in turn provide the raw data out of which our minds construct conscious representations of the external world. Locke was not so naïve as to think that our conscious experiences mirror the world in a particularly literal way. His distinction between primary and secondary qualities that we briefly touched on in Chapter One reveals a relatively high level of scientific sophistication and leaves ample room for psychologists to explain in detail just how our ideas are shaped and the extent to which our minds succeed in accurately reconstructing the world. In this respect, Locke belongs to the empiricist tradition that stretches back to Aristotle. We may quibble with some of the details of Locke's causal theory of perception, as it is called, such as his supposition that at birth one's mind is like a blank slate—the Latin term for this is *tabula rasa*—waiting to be filled with sensory input. This is now regarded as simplistic and out of step with what we know of human neurology, but his general account of our place in the world and of the origins of knowledge remains highly plausible to many philosophers.

A causal theory of knowledge that is quite consistent with Locke derives from the theory of evolution expounded by Charles

Darwin (1809–82). If life in general, and human life in particular, is the product of a long evolutionary process of natural selection, then this has profound implications for the origins, nature and structure of knowledge, since on this account our minds must also be products of the same processes. The emphasis in an evolutionary account of epistemology is on the fitness of our knowledge for our survival as a species. To the extent that we comprise a highly successful species, at least relative to our status as newcomers on the evolutionary stage, our knowledge of the world must also surely be somewhat successful, where success is defined as being at least reliable enough to ensure the propagation of our species. Whenever we look for food, seek shelter, or avoid predators, we obviously rely heavily upon our knowledge of our surroundings to survive. Not all individuals are equally successful survivors and propagators of the species of course, but unless we were more successful than not, we would eventually go the way of the dinosaur. Since our numbers are still increasing, albeit perhaps more rapidly than might be desirable, the argument is that we surely owe this, at least in part, to our knowledge of our environment and our collective ability to master it.

Nothing about a general causal or evolutionary account of knowledge commits us to the view that our knowledge is infallible; indeed Locke goes to great pains to explain how our perceptions of the world diverge from the nature of the world itself. Rather, the emphasis in such theories tends to be on the overall reliability of our knowledge and on suggesting that the explanation of what we know is to be found in the details of our sensory makeup and in our relationship to the environment we inhabit. Theories of this sort also have the virtue of accounting for why we perceive the things we do: our perceptions are what they are because they are caused to be so by our interactions with a world outside our skins. All this is fine as far as it goes, but an interesting problem presents itself when we ask about the reasons we have to believe that such accounts are true. Berkeley realized that a major problem with Locke's theory is that we have no way to compare the similarity of our mental representations of the world with any "external" world precisely because we cannot get outside of our skins. No matter what we do, epistemologically speaking we are stuck with our thoughts and cannot escape them to check whether they really do mirror the outside world.

In the case of evolutionary epistemology this problem takes on an even more interesting wrinkle. If our minds and what they know are products of evolutionary processes, and if biological traits will eventually be selected against if they tend to harm the survival of the species, where does this leave the status of a Darwinian account of epistemology? Ideally, an epistemological theory tells us, among other things, the extent to which our knowledge is indubitable, but in the case of evolutionary epistemology, the most it allows us to conclude is that the beliefs and knowledge we possess have not as yet been selected against. And what about Darwin's theory itself, which is just another one of our beliefs? Is Darwinian theory true? If it is, then an evolutionary account of epistemology does not, in and of itself, appear to provide sufficient grounds to establish this. Again, a Darwinian account of epistemology only goes so far as to lead us to think that belief in Darwinism has not yet been selected against. This weakness is, if not fatal, the Achilles' heel of evolutionary accounts of knowledge.

3.3: KANT'S BIG BREAK

Reading Hume was to have a galvanizing effect on Immanuel Kant, who found the prospect of Humean skepticism so threatening that he fought back at it with an arcane, highly systematic and far-reaching theory of knowledge and cognition. The finer points of Kant's major work, *The Critique of Pure Reason*, are still the subject of lively scholarly debate, and we will content ourselves with no more than a thumbnail sketch of his complex ideas.

Kant's breakthrough consisted in proposing a way to bridge the gulf, bequeathed to him by British empiricists such as Locke, Berkeley, and Hume, between the world on the one hand and our experiences on the other. He did this by rejecting the idea that we are merely passive observers of a pre-existing, outside reality, and also by denying that a simple cause and effect relationship exists between the world and what we know. Rather, Kant thought, we are active participants in the construction of the world as we experience it. How do we do this? Kant argued that we impose upon the jumble of raw sensory inputs certain basic features and in so doing *constitute*, as he put it, the world as we know it. These cognitive structures, or categories, as Kant called them, are so basic and general that we unwittingly assume that they are features of the world itself. Among them are quantity, causality, and the idea of objects as discrete entities. Undifferentiated, raw experience would lack all of these characteristics and be utterly unintelligible, according to Kant, and so our mental categories are not just cognitive tools that conveniently order experience for us, they are the absolutely necessary preconditions of conscious experience itself. To the extent that we can grasp reality at all, Kant thought, we can only understand it in terms of how we structure it.

Instead of inquiring into the way the world is, Kant asked how we participate in constructing the world. Along with Descartes and to some extent Hume and Locke, Kant ushered in a revolution in the history of Western philosophy by subordinating metaphysics to epistemological issues about the scope and limits of knowledge and our cognitive capacities. This is not to say that Kant had no use for metaphysics at all. He accepted the existence of God and was very much a rationalist philosopher. But at the same time he maintained a hard and fast distinction between the world of experience—the *phenomenal* realm, as he called it—and reality as it is independent of experience, which he called the *noumenal* realm. Human experience is wholly confined to phenomena, from which there is no escape, and so strictly speaking we can know and say nothing of the noumenal world, which by definition lies outside experience.

Kant developed his philosophical system well before the advent of Darwin's *The Origin of Species*, but he proved to be prescient in the sense that since his time philosophers and scientists have become much more conscious of the universal cognitive and physiological constraints under which we labour as a species. Kant was not a biologist, but the implications of his conception of the mind are perfectly consistent with evolutionary theory. Biologists examine the nervous systems of various organisms to determine how they are hardwired in the course of evolution, and the idea that neural architecture governs the cognitive capacities of organisms fits neatly with Kant's talk of structures and categories. Noam Chomsky's highly influential theory that structures for generating language are hardwired into our brains builds upon this same philosophical and scientific foundation.

Kant's theory of the universality of categories as preconditions for, and ways of constituting, conscious thought raises fascinating questions about whether other forms of human or non-human consciousness are possible, and if so, whether they are at all conceivable. However, Kant's outlook was somewhat limited and anthropocentric in this area. For example, he regarded flat three-dimensional space—so called Euclidean space—to be the only form that space could conceivably take, apparently for no better reason than that this is the structure space normally appears to have. But as the geometers Riemann, Bolyai, and Lobachevsky later showed, mathematically speaking, curved spaces are perfectly legitimate. While such spaces are difficult to conceptualize, they are by no means impossible to grasp with some concerted effort, Kant's claims to the contrary notwithstanding. In general, there do not seem to be any logical grounds for denying that a being that possesses cognitive machinery significantly different from ours might also have a different form of consciousness from ours, although conceiving alternative forms of consciousness literally beggars the imagination.

By internalizing the notions of knowledge, truth, and reality to our "conceptual schemes," as they are sometimes called in contemporary philosophy, Kant did not deny their existence, but rather held that they can be grasped only within the framework of human understanding. The fundamental shift in philosophy in the direction of epistemology, initiated by Descartes but consolidated by Kant, was to have far-reaching ramifications on succeeding generations of philosophers, so much so that to this day Kantians dismiss modern metaphysicians as doing philosophy as if Kant had never existed.

3.4: Belief and Other Forms of Knowledge

We have said something about the potential sources and origins of knowledge, but as yet we have said little about the structure and content of knowledge. To claim that we know something is to claim we are, or at least can potentially be, in the mental state of being aware of the thing in question. The generic name for such a mental state is belief, and analysis of what beliefs involve takes us a long way toward a more thorough understanding of knowledge. Obviously, not all of our beliefs are present before our minds at any one time, and in fact the vast majority of them remain implicit and forever untapped.

Beliefs bear close and complex relationships to other mental states such as perceptions, memories, and intentions, but we will forego analysis of these connections in this section in order to focus on the links between belief and knowledge. It is in the nature of a belief that it has some sort of content, or object. I say, for example that I believe *that* grass is green, *that* Toronto is in Canada, *that* I have two hands, and so on. Philosophers typically construe this kind of content in quite abstract terms and sometimes refer to it as made up of propositions. I believe that one plus one equals two, and presumably you do as well, but what goes on in your head is different from what goes on in mine, so while our beliefs about the sum of one and one are distinct, they have the same content. In this sense, the justification for the existence of propositions in epistemology is similar to the one we gave in the previous chapter for the existence of abstract propositions in logic. And by the same token, two people standing in a rainstorm can share a belief that it's raining even though they don't speak the same language and so formulate the thought that it's raining in quite different ways.

Some of our beliefs, such as those concerning our immediate surroundings, present themselves to us directly, but, as I mentioned earlier, our beliefs are for the most part implicit. I believe that whales do not eat Cheerios for breakfast, that no downy woodpeckers live on the moon, and that when Michael Jordan was last in Chicago his left ear was in Chicago as well, but I have an inexhaustible supply of other such beliefs that I am unlikely ever to call upon or write down.

The content of a given belief typically relies on prior knowledge and other beliefs. I cannot formulate the belief *Toronto is in Canada*, for example, without already knowing certain things about Toronto, Canada, and what it is for one thing to be "in" something else. Having said that, there is a remote possibility that someone might happen to utter "Toronto is in Canada" without knowing anything about Canada or geography, but then that speaker is at least demonstrating some proficiency with words and grammar in the English language. If a chicken happens to peck out *Toronto is in Canada* on a computer, on the other hand, it exhibits neither beliefs about Canadian geography nor proficiency in English. Even the most basic of beliefs, then, is a relatively high-level cognitive construction, and we typically draw upon a vast number of other beliefs and background knowledge in order to formulate simple beliefs. To sort out which of our beliefs, if any, are more basic or central than others, then, is a difficult task. In light of this, we are probably wise to follow Quine in regarding all our beliefs as constituting a web, although Quine does think that some beliefs, such as those concerning basic principles of logic and mathematics, are more firmly entrenched in the web than others.

On a practical level, beliefs and their contents are highly important because they are the basis for many of our decisions and actions. I reach out for a banana in the fruit bowl on the basis of my antecedent belief that the banana is there. Beliefs figure prominently in other mental states that can also powerfully influence us, such as hopes, desires, aversions, and so on. But what is the relationship between belief and knowledge? For all intents and purposes, we frequently use the words "know" and "believe" interchangeably. To claim to know Paris is the capital of France is not remarkably different from claiming to believe Paris is the capital of France, although depending on the circumstances, the latter may imply that the speaker is less than completely confident in her conviction about the capital of France. A knowledge claim, then, may be regarded as a belief that is well founded, or well supported. Fine, but what is it for a belief to be well supported? The answer philosophers often give is that knowledge consists of beliefs that are adequately *justified*, or *warranted*. Unfortunately, this cannot be the whole story, because we are all familiar with the experience of having had beliefs, even ones we confidently thought were entirely justified, that we later learned were false. Much of the work in epistemology has centered on the nature of justification and the extent to which adequate justification can secure genuine knowledge.

The tradition of characterizing knowledge as justified true belief can be traced at least as far back as Plato's *Theaetetus*, although Plato himself rejected it as an adequate theory of knowledge. Raw perceptions do not count as suitable candidates for real knowledge on this account, since they have not been subjected to the scrutiny or considered judgement that knowledge implies. It is precisely for this reason that scientists subject empirical data to such rigorous review and analysis in building up reliable bodies of scientific knowledge. It is not enough to believe some claim x; we must have good reasons for believing x to assert that we know it. Although much ink has been spilled in the philosophical literature about what constitute adequate criteria for justification and warrant, not to mention the nature of truth, *justified true belief* nevertheless seems to be a worthy and entirely plausible candidate for knowledge, at least at first glance.

However, in a famous paper Edmund Gettier (1927–) argued that justified true belief is not a sufficient criterion for knowledge in all cases. Consider the following example. Suppose you check your watch to find out the time and form the belief that the time is ten past six based on what the watch face indicates. Now suppose that your watch is normally very accurate and that you recently replaced the battery, but that unbeknownst to you, your watch stopped at exactly ten past six yesterday due to some unusual mechanical failure. You haven't checked your watch within the last 24 hours, and so haven't noticed that your watch has stopped. Furthermore, suppose that when you checked your watch, it just happened to be exactly ten past six. What is the status of your belief about what time it is? Your belief that it is ten past six happens to be true, and it is based on your conviction that your watch is reliable, which you are justified in believing. But do you really *know* that it is ten past six? If you think that you do not, your conclusion deals a serious blow to justification and truth as criteria for knowledge and raises questions about what can count as genuine knowledge.

Apart from informed beliefs, knowledge can manifest itself in several other important ways. Much of the knowledge we need to negotiate the world around us is of a practical, skills-based nature. Without acquiring any formal education, we know how to do many things, from riding bicycles to tying shoelaces to figuring out how to select the best watermelon at the supermarket. This "how to" knowledge is by no means inferior or less significant than the cerebral and abstract knowledge of propositions we often think of as more truly exemplifying knowledge. It used to be thought by the pioneers of artificial intelligence that designing machines to solve calculus problems would be very difficult, or at any rate more daunting than building a small robot that would do nothing but move around a room. But we have since discovered to our surprise that designing a machine that knows how to tie shoelaces, butter a slice of bread or maneuver around a living room requires vastly more computing power than empowering it to solve mathematical problems that are beyond the ability of most humans to crack.

There are still other aspects of knowledge that we need to

distinguish. Earlier in this chapter I mentioned that we know some things more directly than others. I know certain facts about the planet Pluto, for instance, which I have never observed, and such knowledge seems to be qualitatively very different from my knowledge that I am currently typing words on my computer or my knowledge that I am not a banana. In *The Problems of Philosophy* Bertrand Russell handled differences of this sort by differentiating between what he called *knowledge by acquaintance* and *knowledge by description*. Roughly speaking, things we are directly aware of, such as immediate perceptions and our introspective thoughts, are known to us by acquaintance, whereas we know facts about Julius Caesar, electrons and, surprisingly, even ordinary physical objects, only indirectly, by description. We do not know Julius Caesar directly, according to Russell, but rather only in terms of descriptions like "the Roman emperor who crossed the Rubicon," but Russell also argues that we are not directly acquainted with physical objects. We are directly acquainted with sense-data of objects, as Russell called them, but these, he says, are not to be confused with the objects themselves. In this respect, Russell followed in the tradition of British empiricists such as Locke and Hume, but his claim that we do not even know each other directly, but only by description, proved to be too counter-intuitive to gain widespread acceptance.

Finally, there is that most elusive and mystifying form of knowledge: intuition. We have all professed to having had hunches, feelings, and insights from time to time that we cannot explain adequately. Sometimes we are right in relying on our "sixth sense," as it is also called, but intuitions can also let us down. Who has not had a feeling of being followed on a dark night, for example, which proved to be wrong, or has not misjudged someone on the basis of an uninformed hunch? As with successful astrological predictions, we tend to make much of intuitions that turn out to be correct, and conveniently ignore cases where our intuitions let us down. Having said that, intuition should not be hastily swept aside or denounced as mere superstition, lucky guesswork, or worse. In fact, intuitions are unavoidable aids to decision-making in philosophy. Some of our basic choices and preferences in philosophy come down to a matter of intuitions rather than definitive proofs, such as whether we are prepared to accept the existence of God. While this might seem frustrating, and for some might even be grounds for avoiding philosophy altogether, perhaps a wiser response would be to acknowledge the central role intuition plays in philosophy and in our lives, and to be as critical as possible whenever we entrust our decision making to intuition.

3.5: Knowledge and/as Information

Profound and far-reaching new technologies have sprung up in recent decades to process, store, and transmit ever-increasing volumes of information. We live in an information age, as the media constantly remind us, but just what is information and how does it relate to knowledge? The burden of this section is to explore these and some related issues.

Information is a highly abstract and technical concept, and its mathematical study belongs to communication theory, developed primarily by the brilliant American engineer Claude Shannon (1916–2001). Information, as Shannon defines it, has to do with the transmission of content from a source to some receptor by means of a signal. A signal operates in some medium, called a channel, and it conveys information. Mathematically speaking, information can be reduced to a series of 0s and 1s, which are called bits. But what kind of thing is information thus construed? A non-technical but nevertheless useful heuristic for thinking about information is to contrast it with what it is not: randomness, which consists in the absence of any meaningful pattern. Informally, then, information may be regarded as any difference that makes a difference. In this very general sense, then, any kind of pattern, order, design or sign of intelligence, no matter how minimal, represents information. Information, in turn, is the foundation upon which knowledge is built. To know something is to be in possession of certain information. So signals convey information, and information conveys knowledge.

Having said this, we should note that not all information amounts to useful knowledge—a truism familiar to many of us who have had bad experiences with information technology. Vast amounts of data can be compiled, duplicated, stored, and recalled via various electronic technologies at our disposal, but this does not mean that all of the information that we accumulate is particularly meaningful or useful. It would be a mistake, however, to lay the blame for useless knowledge entirely at the feet of the information industry. I could, were I so inclined, devote a lot of time and mental energy to memorizing all of the phone numbers on page 135 of the Winnipeg telephone directory. I would acquire knowledge in the process, but the worth of this exercise would be dubious at best. Then there is also misinformation, which can be meaningful but does not strictly speaking constitute knowledge. If I tell you that Edmonton is the capital of Canada, what I say has meaning, but happens to be false. In short, information is a necessary condition of knowledge but not a sufficient condition.

While we have succeeded in compiling more information than any preceding generation in the history of humankind, the sum total of our knowledge has arguably not proliferated to the same degree, although to be fair, information technology has undeniably made access to knowledge more efficient and convenient than ever before. However, the extent to which the recent explosion of information and information technology reflects an increase in wisdom on our part remains debatable. In any case, a significant fragment of our knowledge is informational in nature, and in the next section we will explore the limits of our capacity to grasp knowledge of this kind.

3.6: The Knowable and the Unknowable

Let us return to the task we entertained at the beginning of this chapter: that is, the idea of making a list of all the things we know. We have already noted some of the practical difficulties inherent in such a task, but it presents some problems at the conceptual level as well. In this concluding section, we explore one of these problems. A friendly reminder: the main argument in this section is somewhat technical and is considerably more sophisticated than the rest of the book, so feel free to skip it if you are looking to do introductory level reading only.

While we all claim to know various things, would it be possible for some exceptionally smart person to know everything there is to know? Modesty forbids most of us from making such a presumptuous claim, of course, but what we are interested in here is the logical possibility of human omniscience, not in whether there happen to be some impudent know-it-alls in the world. (A solipsist is someone who believes that he or she is the only thing that exists, and if this just happens to be true of you, dear reader, then you would know everything there is to know because, since in this case there is nothing other than you, there is literally nothing other than you to know. Solipsism cannot be disproved, although we shall consider an argument against it in the concluding chapter, but aside from infants and the acutely autistic, sincere solipsists are thin on the ground.)

If we are honest, then, we will admit that we do not know everything and include on our list of the things we know the entry: "I know that I do not know everything." I happen to know nothing about how to read Sanskrit, the exact population of Uzbekistan, what it is like to orbit the earth in the space shuttle, and many other things. Having admitted that these are things I do not know, obviously there is little else I can say about them. But leaving aside "knowing how" and experiential knowledge for the time being and restricting ourselves to "knowing that" knowledge, let us consider whether there can be anything that *no one* knows. Either human minds collectively comprehend everything there is to be known, or there are things to be known that forever lie beyond the grasp of humans. Do we have reason to think there is any such thing, and if so, is there anything we can say about the things that no one knows? I develop an argument below in which, relative to certain key assumptions, the answer to both these questions is yes, although naturally the most we can say is *that* we do not know certain things rather than say explicitly what it is we don't know (in which case it would be known to us). The assumptions upon which the argument is based are that the human mind is finite and that all that we know and indeed can know is expressible in written form. I return to the first of these assumptions later.

The argument is adapted from a discussion of Richard's Paradox by Rudy Rucker (1946–) in his book *Infinity and the Mind*. Written language consists of finite strings of symbols that can be combined in various ways to express our thoughts, ideas, and knowledge. Suppose that we were to gather together all human knowledge, past, present, and future, in all human languages, into one vast database. This database would include all of the books, notes, unfinished manuscripts, manuals, recipes, journals, diaries, letters, and even shopping lists that have been, will be, or even could be written down. It would also include tediously long, painstaking lists of what every person, past, present, and future, has ever known. Now as massive an amount of information as this is, it is, to use a concept we will discuss in Chapter Five, countably infinite; and it can be encoded by a single, fantastically large number. How would this coding work? Leaving out the numbers 0, 1, 10, and 20 for reasons I will explain shortly, we could assign the numbers 2–29 to all of the 26 lower-case letters in English respectively. Then, leaving out 40 and 50, we could assign the numbers 31–58 to the upper case English letters and assign other numbers to punctuation marks such as "?" and ";" always leaving out numbers containing zero. We could then extend this coding system to all languages containing alphabets, punctuation marks, and ideographs that differ from English. All of this would require roughly ten to fifteen thousand zero-less numbers. We reserve the number one for the spaces between words, which are really a kind of punctuation mark, and the number zero to act as a spacer between code numbers themselves. Although we have not written down this coding system in full here, you should be able to satisfy yourself without too much trouble that the word "cat" comes out as the code number 402023, where the zeroes separate 4, 2, and 23, which in turn are the code numbers corresponding to "c," "a," and "t" respectively. The phrase "this book" translates as the code number 23090110220101030170170113. Notice that the sequence 010 always corresponds to the space between words or ideographs. Obviously the numbers encoding even short sentences are quite large, not to mention the code number for, say, an encyclopaedia. Note also that the code numbers for the French, English, and Russian versions of the same encyclopaedia would differ from one another. Fortunately numbers are in such plentiful supply that running out of them is not a problem.

Now as large as these individual code numbers can become, we can still count them one by one. And if we string together all of these individual code numbers into one enormous number that encodes all human knowledge expressible in written form, we get an infinitely long master number—call it M—but still one that we could in principle reach by counting. Why is M infinite? To appreciate why, note that it would have to embed not only the code number for "zero is a number," but also the code number for "one is a number," the code number for "two is a number," and so on, ad infinitum. Fortunately, the so-called real numbers, of which more in Chapter Five, are a convenient source of the number M. M, then, is a single, infinitely long real number. There is no unique way to order the sum total of human knowledge in written form, but if we were to start out like this: *Grass is green, and Calgary is in Canada, and* ..., then the number M would begin: 370210202202201011022010802106060160 ..., where 37 encodes "G" and M extends as far as the last letter of "green," which is encoded by 16.

Now nothing about alphabet letters, words, and spaces makes them superior to digits; they are just different means by which we can represent knowledge symbolically. Since we are supposing that all human knowledge can be encoded using individual code numbers conjoined together to generate M, we can see that M is one gigantic numerical representation of all human knowledge. We could, were we so inclined, even train ourselves to communicate in this new, numerical language of code-numbers. Regardless, the point is that by definition, M represents all human knowledge in all human languages, and so in principle M encodes all knowledge that is available to humans. Right? Wrong!

To appreciate why M is not and cannot be all that it's cracked up to be, we first need to specify another real number, called the diagonal of M, or d_M, which is different from M and which will never appear anywhere in the endless expanse of M. What is this number d_M? We generate d_M by changing the first digit of M, which in our version of M is a 3, into another digit, 4. We then change the second digit of M, which is 7, into another digit, 8; we change the third digit of M, which is 0, into 1, and so on. In other words, we define d_M to be the number we get when we add one to each digit of M respectively, and change each of the nines in M to zeroes. The result is that for any number n, d_M is constructed in such a way that its nth digit is different from the nth digit of M. So now we have a new real number, d_M, which begins: 481..., designed specifically and for no other purpose than to differ from M. (Strictly speaking, I have not defined the diagonal of M in the same way or as rigorously as diagonalization is understood by mathematicians and logicians; rather, my point is to use a crude version of diagonalization to expose the limitations of countable systems to represent or encode everything there is to be known.)

Now the number d_M does not necessarily encode anything intelligible; it is simply a number that by definition differs from M. But to learn the number d_M *would* constitute another piece of knowledge, corresponding to a statement beginning something like this: "I know the number 481...." Would learning d_M help us complete our inventory of all knowledge and thereby help us to perfect M? The answer is *no*. This new piece of knowledge, "I know the number 481...," would have to have its own code number—call it $CODEd_M$. Inserting or adding $CODEd_M$ to M

would generate a new, "improved" master number M^+, but M^+ would allow us simply to generate a new diagonal number d_{M+}. In any case, the very idea of inserting or adding $CODEd_M$ to M is suspect. Remember, our original idea was that M supposedly represents everything there is to be known, but if M needed supplementing with $CODEd_M$, this would mean either that M wasn't living up to its job description in the first place, or else that $CODEd_M$ is not something that M was capable of encoding in the first place. Either way, we have to conclude that there is really no such thing as M after all! Finally, notice that M *can* encode the sentence "There is a number called the diagonal of M which M cannot encode." This sentence expresses something we *do* know, and so the code number for this sentence *would* appear somewhere in M.

To sum up, we have shown that there is a number d_M that lies beyond the reach of M and cannot therefore be encoded by M, even though by definition M is supposed to encode everything we know. M does not encode the code number $CODEd_M$, because d_M is beyond the reach of M. So either d_M and its code number $CODEd_M$ are known to us, in which case M does not encode everything after all, or there is no such thing as M to begin with. We can specify how to construct d_M precisely on the basis of M, however, and so we are forced to conclude that M is a fiction. In short, while we can know all sorts of things, we cannot know everything. This should not come as a huge surprise; we have, after all, a passing acquaintance with the barest minimum of numbers. The paradox, however, lies in the fact that we can prove there must always be at least one real number beyond our grasp, not only because real numbers are very difficult to wrap our heads around in practice, but because it is impossible to grasp all of them in principle.

Returning to the original point of my argument, which is that there are things we cannot know, does the above argument show that any *specific* number is unknowable? Not at all; we can know any given real number that we care to specify to any arbitrary extent. The problem is not that we do not know d_M or $CODEd_M$ or any other *specific* number with arbitrary precision. The problem is simply that we cannot know all of the real numbers, and that therefore we cannot know everything. As I mentioned above, this argument is based on certain premises, and if one or more of those premises is false, the argument is unsound. One of these premises is that what we know can be expressed in written form. Obviously, this condition is required to get the idea of a coding system off the ground. But even if there are forms of knowledge other than those that are expressible in language, that doesn't undermine our argument, since we have only established that there are some areas of knowledge beyond our grasp. The other assumption, that our minds are finite, is somewhat trickier. We have a finite number of brain cells, our life spans are finite in duration and we cannot, at least according to Zeno, whom we will revisit in Chapter Five, perform an infinite number of tasks in a finite amount of time. On the other hand, there is something mysterious about the way we seem to be able to grasp notions of infinity and infinite processes intuitively. Consider the way we are able to appreciate the idea of the infinite regress of reflections we see when we step into a room with mirrors on opposing walls. We seem to be able to reflect ourselves at a cognitive level, in that we can realize we exist, realize that we realize we exist, realize that we realize that we realize we exist, and so on. Our perennial fascination with the infinite and our need to theorize about it in physics, mathematics, religion, and philosophy are tantalizing reasons to suggest that our minds may not be finite after all. How to reconcile the apparent tension between our physical finitude on the one hand and our affinity for the infinite on the other remains one of the most fascinating of philosophy's perennial problems.

Be that as it may, an entity with an infinite mind might somehow be able to grasp all human knowledge, past, present, and future, including the numbers M and d_M, at once. To a being possessing an infinite intelligence—God, in essence—all of this knowledge would be available. But even though we are endowed with astonishingly complex brains, we have only a finite numbers of brain cells; and for mere mortals like ourselves to claim that we are omniscient or have infinite knowledge surely gives us too much credit. In all likelihood, whatever knowledge we are capable of acquiring is destined to remain neither completely reliable nor complete. As pessimistic as this conclusion appears, we do well not to lose sight of it, for therein lies something even more important than knowledge: namely wisdom.

CHAPTER 4

Ethics:
Values and Virtues

Live pure, speak true, right wrong.

— ALFRED, LORD TENNYSON

4.0: INTRODUCTION

How should we conduct ourselves and how should we treat others? What is morally right and wrong, and what is the nature of the things we designate morally good and bad? Are such things absolute and eternal, or are they strictly relative, reflections merely of the standards or values of various societies or individuals? Is morality important only as far as behavior is concerned, or is it also a matter of what we think, or of our principles? What constitutes a good life? Should we extend moral consideration to species other than our own, and if so, why? What is important to us and why? Is there anything ultimately worth living or dying for, or are our lives essentially meaningless? Questions such as these preoccupy many of us, not just professional ethicists. In a sense these issues are practical in nature, for no matter who we are or what we do, we all have a vested interest in living a worthy and successful life. Indeed, in some philosophical traditions, such as China's, the subject of ethics has historically been the main focus of philosophy. In this chapter, we take up some of the above questions and consider answers to them by way of a tour of some prominent ethical theories.

The recognition and observance of a distinction between good and evil or between right and wrong is a basic organizational principle upon which all societies are based. However, the ways in which such distinctions are drawn and observed appear to vary significantly from one society to another. Are there any commonalities underlying these apparent differences between societies? Before we can begin to address questions such as these and the ones in the opening paragraph, we first need to say something about the language of moral discourse and how it differs from other areas of inquiry.

4.1: FACTS, VALUES, AND THE LANGUAGE OF ETHICS

Philosophical concepts are nothing if not slippery and abstract, and this is especially true in the area of moral philosophy, where many of the concepts under consideration have deeply personal and subjective overtones. To appreciate this, consider how factual language differs from language that expresses values.

Many, but by no means all, philosophers agree that there is a fundamental difference between statements of fact and statements of value and that one kind of statement cannot be reduced to the other. Facts are statements that purport to express truths, where these statements are, in principle at least, objectively true or false. For example, the following sentences are all factual in nature, in the sense that they are, at least in principle, objectively true or false:

Calgary is a city in Alberta.

Table salt consists of sodium and chlorine.

All mammals require oxygen to live.

There are at least ten million rocks on the surface of Mars.

Some facts can be verified in practice, while some others can be verified only in principle. It is relatively easy to verify that Calgary is a city in Alberta, but not necessarily so easy to verify claims about specific numbers of rocks on other planets. To claim that there are at least ten million rocks on the surface of Mars is at present very difficult to verify, although it is in principle possible to do so. Whether or not all facts are at least potentially verifiable is a controversial question in philosophy, but one that we can safely ignore for present purposes. Note also that some statements of fact may be true at some times but not at others. "Calgary is a city of over 500,000 people" is one such statement, while some statements that purport to express facts turn out to be false. "All swans are white," for example, was assumed to be true for a long time until black swans were discovered, while the statement "Calgary is a city in the South Pacific" purports to express a fact but is false.

Compare such statements with the following, all of which express values of one sort or another:

Government spending on education is more important than debt reduction.

Chocolate tastes much better than vanilla.

Brian Mulroney was the best prime minister in Canadian history.

We should do more to relieve the suffering of animals.

Values are difficult to define precisely, but one can get a sense of what values are by asking oneself what kinds of things might count as being important. Are there ways to determine whether value-laden statements are objectively true? Whether or not we agree with individual value statements, there appears no easy way to settle whether such claims are true or false, nor whether this would be possible even in principle. If not, then we appear to be stuck with a basic dichotomy between factual and value-laden claims.

Having asserted that there is a dichotomy between facts and values, I should hasten to add that we often attempt to resolve disagreements between people based on values by attempting to clarify value-laden claims and reducing them to facts. For example, if I were to argue that Acme makes terrible computers, a quite natural response to this would be to ask, "What do you mean by the word 'terrible'?" Now suppose I were to go on and define the criteria I have in mind when I refer to a computer as terrible, which might include, say, slow processing speeds, unreliable performance, poor after-sales service, and so on. What I am doing is attempting to translate my value-laden claim into factual terms. Of course this does not mean that anyone else agrees with my judgment of Acme computers as terrible, since anyone is free to reject or dispute my criteria. Whether all value-laden language, and indeed all of ethics, can be grounded in facts is a highly controversial and important question. Without entering into this debate here, I should say that I doubt that values will be dispensed with and replaced entirely by facts any time soon.

Whatever may be the status of statements that express values, values play an all-important role in our lives. Directly or indirectly, they motivate virtually all that we do, and an appreciation of the ways in which values shape our lives is absolutely essential to any kind of philosophical or psychological understanding of who and what we are as humans. Even the fact that you are currently reading these words is an expression of at least some of your values. You could be watching television or swimming or playing video games or doing any number of other things with your time instead, but the fact that you are reading these words indicates that you have some interest in what I write, which in turn reflects one or more of your values. Perhaps you value academic pursuits or the judgment of someone who recommended this book to you. Maybe you are reading this book because I begged you to. Whatever the case, the point is that our values dictate much of what we do. Capitalists value money and the accumulation of personal wealth, artists value creativity, pro-choice advocates in the abortion debate place a higher value on a woman's right to choose an abortion than on the rights of her fetus, and so on.

We also exhibit our values whenever we pass *value judgments*. "Wanda is a great singer" and "Joe is a lousy manager" are value judgments, as is "You should donate more money to charity." There is a subset of value judgments that is of special relevance to this chapter: those judgments that dictate how we should or ought to behave. Such statements are called *prescriptive*, or *normative*. We might agree that Wayne Gretzky is not an outstanding chemist nor Nobel Prize material as a medical researcher, but in passing such judgments we are not necessarily suggesting that he *should* take up chemistry or brain surgery. After all, he was a brilliant hockey player who has devoted most of his life to perfecting his hockey skills, and we understand that this precluded him from excelling in most other fields. But if we were to assert that Gretzky should spend more time with his family or that rich hockey players ought to donate more of their money to support junior hockey, then we are making prescriptive claims.

Closely related to the fact-value dichotomy is the so-called "is-ought" fallacy, first articulated by David Hume. In a previous chapter we discussed arguments, validity, and what it means for a conclusion to follow from premises. Now if the fact-value dichotomy is real, then the question arises: Can value-laden statements follow from factual premises? More precisely, do prescriptive, or "ought"-type, statements follow from factual, or "is"-type, premises? Consider the following argument, which consists of a single premise and a conclusion:

The government of Rwanda tortures and executes political prisoners.

Therefore Canada ought to impose economic sanctions on Rwanda.

From a strictly logical point of view, and disregarding whether the premise is true, does the conclusion necessarily follow from the premise? Clearly it does not. As Hume observed, no number of facts about the world around us can lead us to moral conclusions, including conclusions about what should or should not be done about those facts. To think otherwise is the *is-ought fallacy*. But does this mean that reasoning breaks down altogether when it comes to ethics and that we cannot construct *any* arguments leading to moral conclusions? Not quite, for all the "is-ought" fallacy really implies is that we need to be very careful to make explicit the often implicit moral assumptions we make when we argue for moral conclusions. To understand this, consider the following argument, which differs from the previous one with respect to the addition of a key premise only:

The government of Rwanda executes political prisoners.

All nations ought to impose economic sanctions on governments that execute political prisoners.

Therefore Canada ought to impose economic sanctions on Rwanda.

Given these two premises, the conclusion does follow from the premises now, but this is only because we inserted a relevant, prescriptive premise into the argument.

Broadly speaking, there are two main kinds of theories in ethics: *descriptive* and *prescriptive* theories. Descriptive theories are concerned with what morals and ethics are, how they arise and how they actually function in the lives of individuals and societies. In a sense, the role of a descriptive ethicist is somewhat similar to that of an anthropologist or sociologist who studies the principles upon which societies are organized and attempts to describe their codes, customs, practices, and systems of behavior in a detached, scientific manner. Prescriptive theories of ethics, on the other hand, aim to tell us how we should, or ought to, behave. Needless to say, theories of this latter type, some of which we will discuss shortly, tend to generate controversy and heated debate, but they are important in spite of this. Indeed, the fact that such theories are capable of stirring people's passions is perhaps evidence of their significance.

Before ending this section on language and ethics, I should say something about the words "ethics" and "morals." In everyday language these two words are often used interchangeably, but in philosophy they differ slightly in meaning. In its adjectival form, "moral" is typically used to refer to specific, prescriptive rules, principles or behaviors, whereas "ethics" is used in a more general sense to describe entire theories, codes and systems of conduct, both prescriptive and descriptive. But this distinction is not absolutely hard and fast, and little turns on demarcating strictly between these two words.

4.2: CULTURAL DIFFERENCES AND ETHICAL RELATIVISM

No one who travels widely, studies social sciences such as anthropology or sociology, or lives in a multicultural society for any length of time can fail to be struck by the myriad differences that exist between people, both within and among different cultures. These differences, which encompass traditions, customs, rituals, rites, practices, ceremonies, conventions, taboos, and many other aspects of human behavior, are grist for the mill for social scientists, and, to the extent that they influence ethics, relevant to descriptive ethics as well. But what do cultural differences have to teach ethicists, and how should they inform our thinking about prescriptive ethics? Let us investigate these questions by first considering some examples of cultural differences.

The implications for ethics of differences between societies vary significantly. Consider as an example one major difference regarding conventions to do with driving motor vehicles. In England, Australia, and some other countries, cars are fitted with steering wheels on the right-hand side and motorists drive on the left-hand side of the road, whereas in North America and Europe the steering wheel is on the left-hand side of vehicles and drivers keep to the right. These conventions have long since become entrenched as laws enforceable by police and the courts. Motorists everywhere are expected to abide by the laws in force in their respective countries, but the point is that there is nothing morally superior about one convention as opposed to the other; they are simply different ways of organizing traffic.

However, things get murky when we consider social phenomena such as customs, religious practices, and cultural traditions. What may be a perfectly respectable and morally acceptable behavior in one culture or society may be treated with indifference, frowned upon or even actively proscribed in others, depending on their contexts and a host of personal, social, political, and religious variables. Ordinarily, the wearing of turbans by male Sikhs is an uncontroversial practice, but it has created resentment among some Canadians concerned about the image of the RCMP if its officers are allowed to wear turbans. A more serious issue concerns female circumcision, which is still practiced in some African communities but is rejected as barbaric in many other societies. Issues such as these are more than just minor social irritants for countries that promote multiculturalism; they have social, national, and international ramifications. And even more morally charged actions are those purposely designed to violate taboos, such as incest, infanticide or pederasty.

Then there is the thorny question of the role that genetics plays in determining our behavior. On a purely biological level, a human individual is an expression—or *phenotype*, to use the biological term—of his or her genetic makeup. How far this genetic programming extends into cognitive and moral realms is a matter of intense debate in the social and biological sciences. The recently fashionable theory of sociobiology not only proposes that our moral behavior can in principle be understood in genetic terms, but goes so far as to advocate that ethics should be informed by our rapidly expanding knowledge of human biology. Proponents of this view would argue, for example, that if homosexuality is grounded in facts about human biology, we should accept it as such in our moral reckoning.

Given that close and complex interrelationships exist between ethics and the many cultural differences between individuals and societies, the question arises: Is ethics entirely explicable in terms of facts about human society, culture or genetics? Alternatively, can we explain ethics, particularly differences in moral standards between people, entirely in terms of the ways these differences express themselves socially, culturally or genetically? We are not inquiring here into how human beings *should* behave; rather, we are asking very general questions about the description of ethics.

If all of ethics is wholly determined by some combination of social, cultural or genetic variables, then we must accept that specific ethical principles and systems apply to individuals and cultures only relative to those particular variables. It follows from this that there are not necessarily any universal moral rights or wrongs; changes in social, cultural or genetic factors can change the relevant moral standards, no matter how cherished or repugnant those standards might be. Indeed, this is precisely what ethical relativists would have us believe. Sincere relativists must tolerate the entire spectrum of behaviors and standards when it comes to morality, even if those standards differ wildly from their own, because relativists accept such differences at face value as arising from particular environmental or individual conditions. In general, sensitivity and tolerance concerning individual and cultural differences is surely a good thing, so what, if anything, is wrong with ethical relativism? Here are some reasons for not going all the way with ethical relativism.

Tolerance towards others is a virtue, but tolerance of absolutely anything is not something that is commonly practiced, nor is it even particularly desirable. A systematic ethical relativist must concede that she has no more than *relative* grounds for condemning rape, torture, the murder of innocent children or any other wicked act. This is because, having given up on moral absolutes, she is left without a real yardstick or standard against which to condemn any act as immoral. I doubt that extreme tolerance of this sort is compatible with our sense of humanity, however, and it may even be humanly impractical as a way of life. It may well be that relative to one set of assumptions abortion is acceptable, but that relative to another set of assumptions it is not. However, it is a contradiction to claim that abortion is both acceptable *and* unacceptable, period. What we happen to think about the acceptability of abortion is not the point here; the point is that logicians generally regard contradictions to be intolerable. Unless the relativist claims that moral questions have answers *only* relative to certain assumptions, it would appear that she is stuck with contradictions.

Ethical relativism comes at a huge cost. It requires us to sacrifice our shared sense of humanity, which tends to make normal people recoil at the idea of remaining sanguine about, say, vicious crimes. And it asks us to deny our instinctive aversion to contradictions unless we evade direct answers to questions such as "Is female genital mutilation morally acceptable?" We revisit relativism and its implications briefly towards the end of the book, but for now we will turn from issues concerning ethics in general to specific theories about making moral decisions and how we should live our lives, beginning with utilitarian ethics.

4.3: UTILITARIAN ETHICS

One of the most influential of modern ethical theories, utilitarian ethics, originated with two English philosophers, Jeremy Bentham (1748–1832) and John Stuart Mill (1806–73). The *milieu* of Mill and Bentham, both of whom also made important contributions to social and political philosophy, was one in which modern liberal ideals of equality and individual rights were being propagated throughout the English-speaking world, but also one in which nation states were able to exercise increasing levels of power and control over individuals. The tension between these trends is very much evident in the theory of ethics that is their most enduring legacy.

The basis of utilitarian ethics is the *utility principle*, one version of which states that when faced with making a moral decision we should act in such a way as to bring about the greatest happiness for the greatest number. Several features of this principle warrant discussion. First, the theory emphasizes happiness as the morally desirable outcome of our actions. In general, the aim of prescriptive theories of ethics is to determine what is good for individuals or society at large, but not surprisingly, the basic differences between such theories tend to stem from different conceptions of just what the good *is* and how best to achieve it. For utilitarians, actions are good to the extent that they maximize overall happiness or minimize overall pain.

The utility principle implicitly recognizes that our actions admit of *degrees* of happiness and pain, and also that there are degrees in terms of the numbers of people affected by our various actions. This seems straightforward enough, but more problematic are questions about the sources and quality of the pleasures we experience. Is the quality of happiness a teenager derives from, say, listening to gangsta rap comparable to the pleasure her grandparents acquire from the opera, which they have come to appreciate deeply over the course of many years? And if so, in what sense are they comparable? Are some pleasures, in other words, superior to others? A couch potato who is content simply to watch hockey on television might claim, perhaps quite justifiably, to be happier than a philosopher who spends a lifetime tackling difficult questions without resolving them, but does this mean that a life spent watching television is worthier than a philosopher's? As we shall see below, this problem is no mere academic debate, but presents many practical problems in the real world of political decision making. Mill was well aware of this difficulty and, unlike Bentham, differentiated between what he thought were higher and baser pleasures. While we might at first be motivated by the urge to satisfy our simple pleasures, Mill thought that we can also come to acquire nobler motives, such as promoting human welfare, and that we can find the pursuit of such motives to be pleasurable and ends in themselves. However, critics reply that Mill is simply appointing himself as an arbiter of taste and being an elitist. In addition, its emphasis on the maximization of pleasure renders utilitarian ethics too hedonistic for some critics.

The utility principle does not require us to ignore our own desires or preferences. The point is rather that we need to factor in the desires or preferences of the majority with our own when we make moral choices. Ideally, our own wants and desires are consistent with those of the majority, in which case we are free to satisfy our desires, but the theory dictates that the utility of the majority trumps that of the individual. It is here that the democratic and egalitarian aspects of utilitarianism become clearly evident. In a democratic election, everyone is free to vote for the political party of his or her choice, but the true democrat accepts the outcome of elections based on the principle of majority rule, even if the majority elects a party different from the one that the democrat supports. Of course, the ideal situation for democrats and utilitarians alike is that the wishes of the majority are consistent with their own, in which case the result is a "win-win" scenario, but the principle in both cases is that the voice of the majority must prevail over that of the minority. Also of fundamental importance to both democrats and utilitarians is that the decision-making process is based on the principle of equality.

Finally, utilitarians stress that it is the *consequences* of our actions that are morally significant, not necessarily the actions in and of themselves. As long as the overall result of an action is to increase happiness or decrease pain, it is morally desirable in terms of this theory. The use of utilitarian reasoning is widespread, not only at a personal level but also at the level of the civil service, hospital boards, management teams, and other authorities charged with making ethical choices affecting the lives of others, particularly where those choices are constrained by limited resources. Now let us consider how this theory might apply to a situation requiring some real-world decision making.

Suppose you are a local politician serving on a committee whose job it is to make recommendations to the city regarding a public works project. Suppose, furthermore, that your committee has narrowed down the choice for this project to one of two alternatives: an art gallery and a junior hockey rink. If you were to take a utilitarian approach to help you decide which of these options to support, you would presumably base your decision on what the majority of the local population wants, reasoning that this strategy should bring about the greatest happiness for the greatest number. Now suppose that you try to determine the wishes of the people by conducting a poll, for example, or by holding a plebiscite. Furthermore, suppose the results show that 60 per cent of the population would prefer the hockey rink, while 40 per cent favor the art gallery. Fine. You urge the committee to recommend construction of the hockey rink, and the decision is announced to the public.

But now suppose that rather than meeting with general support, your committee's decision draws vigorous opposition from scores of outraged citizens, who organize protests, write letters to the city and the local newspapers expressing their outrage with the decision, and demand that the committee reverse its decision. What has gone wrong? A likely explanation is that the protests emanate from the 40 per cent minority, and that the trouble with your decision is that you have failed to take into account the strength of their preference. That is to say, it is likely that the minority of people in favor of the arts centre have a very strong preference for the arts centre, while the majority might have only a mild preference for the junior hockey rink. What to do?

Problems of this sort are quite familiar to any democratically minded politician who genuinely tries to satisfy the wishes of the people, and there are no easy solutions to these dilemmas. Often, decisions regarding construction projects, mining developments, logging proposals, and so on, are affected and sometimes even overturned due to strong opposition from local landowners or well-organized environmental lobby groups. The general problem here is that it is difficult to compare and quantify the various desires and preferences people may have. How do we compare the pleasure one person derives from art to another person's love of hockey? How do we weigh the convenience some commuters might derive from the construction of a new road with the pain caused to a family whose farmhouse will be bulldozed if the road is constructed? Is the protection of an endangered species of owl more important than the economic boost a struggling rural community would derive from a new logging operation? Utilitarian reasoning is predicated on the assumption that people's interests, values, and preferences can somehow be compared, quantified, and reduced to a kind of numbers game, but alas real people are not always accommodating enough for this theory to work well in practice.

We have already encountered one problem with utilitarian ethics, but there are others. The theory stresses that it is the consequences of our actions, rather than the actions themselves, that count in our moral reckoning, but the consequences of our actions are not always foreseeable. Environmental disasters often result from just this problem. A mining project that might promise beneficial, short-term economic and political consequences may eventually generate detrimental, unforeseen and long-term environmental consequences.

Moreover, what should we say of someone who models himself on Robin Hood, stealing from the rich and giving to the poor, while defending his actions on the basis that he is attempting to maximize overall happiness in society by taking money from a handful of rich people and giving it to the poor masses? Anyone who feels uncomfortable with this line of reasoning and is inclined to view theft as morally unjustifiable—even if it is committed in the name of social justice—thereby objects to the utilitarian rationale of Robin Hood.

And finally, if the point of our moral decision-making is to satisfy the desires of the majority, how should we regard a society in which the majority of people derive pleasure from policies most of us would consider to be perverse, corrupt, racist, or otherwise abhorrent? Unsavory examples spring all too readily to mind: Nazi Germany, the brutal regime of the Khmer Rouge in Cambodia, apartheid-era South Africa, and so on. If the majority of people in such societies defend the violence, racism, or oppression on the basis of the utility principle, should we accept their desires as legitimate?

If not, then we are implicitly rejecting utilitarian reasoning, at least as far as I have characterized it.

Proponents of utilitarianism parried objections of the sort we have raised here virtually from the time of the theory's inception. The original, pure form of the theory goes by the name of *act* utilitarian ethics, and a refinement of it deals with the last of these objections. The refinement goes by the name of *rule* utilitarian ethics, which involves the application of utilitarian reasoning not to actions, but rather to a set of rules—for example, laws against theft, racism, and other forms of discrimination. This modification is meant to protect us from the potential injustices allowed for by the original form of the theory, but the problem with this rule utilitarian alternative is that there is ultimately nothing to prevent the majority from rescinding those rules at any point and reverting to the application of the utility principle in its original form.

Interpreting the utility principle depends crucially on the meaning of the phrase "the greatest number," as the principle leaves unclear exactly who or what "the greatest number" refers to. Does it extend only as far as the members of one's local community, to everyone in the world, or even to non-human animals? If utilitarians are concerned with promoting happiness and relieving pain and suffering in the world, and assuming that animals such as cats, dogs, cows, and sheep are capable of experiencing pain, then perhaps we should take all sentient beings into account in our utilitarian reasoning. Bentham embraced this consequence as a virtue and thought that we should indeed extend the theory to other sentient beings. Some modern-day utilitarians, most notably Peter Singer (1946–), have developed this line of reasoning into a sophisticated defense of animal rights and a vegetarian lifestyle. Their arguments gain force if we pause to consider how we ourselves would want to be treated in the following hypothetical situation. Suppose advanced aliens invade the earth, holding us captive, and suppose they are able to survive perfectly well by eating either inanimate matter such as rocks or carbon-based organisms such as ourselves. Wouldn't we want them to choose rocks for breakfast instead of us? And if we were somehow able to reason with these aliens, wouldn't we all be ardent utilitarians and want them to show exactly the same sort of empathy towards us that utilitarians like Singer exhibit toward animals? Questions such as these form the basis of some of the contemporary debates about utilitarian ethics.

4.4: Kantian Ethics

A very different but also highly influential theory of ethics is the one articulated by the great German philosopher Immanuel Kant.

As with utilitarianism, Kant's ethical system can also be encapsulated in a principle, which in this case is the *universalizability principle*. This principle states that, faced with making a moral choice, one should act in such a way that one's own action could become a universal moral law. In other words, what you choose to do in any given situation should be such that you would find it acceptable for anyone to do in a similar situation. But if that action affects other people and if it's acceptable for anyone else to do, then it follows that you would have to find it acceptable for that action to be done to you. This is reminiscent of the Golden Rule, which states: *Do unto others as you would have them do unto you.* What Kant's principle shares with the Golden Rule is the concept of reversibility: the idea that an action affecting someone else is acceptable only if the parties involved would still tolerate the action if the roles were reversed. Interestingly, versions of the Golden Rule appear in most major religions.

But while the Golden Rule relies solely on the test of reversibility, Kant's theory is meant to be more general in the sense that it is meant to compel us on purely rational grounds. For example, Kant's theory rules out lying, cheating, stealing, and harming others, because no one wants to be lied to, cheated, stolen from or harmed, at least not if one is rational. The universalizability principle is also more general than the Golden Rule because it does not require that anyone else be involved. Suppose you are a passenger on an airplane when it develops engine trouble at 30,000 feet and goes into a steep nose-dive. In your desperation, you make a solemn promise to donate half of your assets to charity if you survive the crash, a promise heard by none of the other screaming passengers. Now suppose that you miraculously survive the crash, but upon recalling your vow and realizing no one else heard it, you renege on your promise. Is your change of heart morally problematic? There is no one with which to reverse roles in this situation, but a Kantian regards reneging on a promise to be morally unacceptable in itself. The reason is that the principle that is involved here—breaking a promise—is not universalizable, at least not according to Kant. If everyone broke his or her promise, then making promises would be pointless, and so for Kantians it cannot be rational to break a promise, regardless of the circumstances. Of course, you might object that the principle that is really at stake here is breaking a promise *that no one hears*, and that violating *that* principle is benign.

The airplane example conveniently illustrates some other features of Kant's theory. Kant takes actions to be right or wrong in and of themselves; and he thinks we have a duty to do the right thing for its own sake, irrespective of whatever personal rewards might accrue from doing so, whether others are aware of the action, and regardless of the consequences of the action. Furthermore, Kant emphasizes that having a good will, or the right intention, is what really counts when it comes to our moral decision making. This contrasts starkly with utilitarians, for whom it is the consequences of actions that matter, and for whom having one's heart in the right place is irrelevant if one's actions end up causing more harm than good.

According to Kant's conception of ethics, it is ultimately only individual humans who are accountable, and to whom we are accountable, in our moral deliberations. We cannot ever use others as means to our own ends; to use Kant's jargon, people are "ends in themselves." Careful consideration of the meaning of reversibility should make this clear. Suppose you are tempted to do something that involves taking advantage of someone else.

Reversibility would force you to accept that this implies you would have to allow yourself to be taken advantage of by the other person if the roles were reversed. But since no one would really want to be taken advantage of, it follows that you are not justified in taking advantage of another person in the first place.

Kant's universalizability principle is relatively easy to understand, powerful, and relevant in a wide range of situations. Are you entitled to cut in to the front of a lineup of people at a grocery checkout? No, according to this theory, because you would have to take into account how you would feel if you were one of the people in the lineup, and no rational person is willing to be exploited in this way. But this theory also has its drawbacks. While the universalizability principle is relatively easy to grasp, it is perhaps too uncompromising to warrant slavish obedience at all times. Consider lying, for example. Generally speaking, it is good to be honest and avoid telling lies, but who hasn't told the occasional white lie in order to prevent someone's feelings from being hurt? If you receive a gift you really don't like from a close relative, it would hardly be gracious of you to admit your true feelings about the gift if the relative asks you whether you like it. In putting principles before human sensibilities, Kant's theory would seem to be too onerous in certain cases.

Telling the truth might also conflict with other duties we might have. Kant assumes that the universalizability principle will always dictate to us the rational and morally correct course of action to take, but it is doubtful that the theory can always deliver on this. Consider a doctor caring for an elderly patient in very frail health. Suppose the doctor has just received some test results suggesting that the prognosis for the patient is extremely poor. The doctor has a professional and humanitarian duty to act in the best interests of her patient's health, but also a Kantian duty to tell the truth, and if the doctor determines that explaining the test results to her patient would only worsen his condition, then her duties conflict. What should the doctor do? Unfortunately, Kantian ethics does not offer us an answer.

Finally, Kant's theory is predicated on the assumption that

humans are rational, and it breaks down if not everyone thinks rationally. It is not rational to want to be harmed, tortured or killed, for example, but sadly not everyone is entirely rational. To appreciate the consequences of this point for Kantian ethics, imagine confronting a Nazi torturing a Jew during World War II and challenging the morality of his actions by appealing to the universalizability principle. That is to say, one might object to the Nazi: "How can you justify torturing a Jew? After all, how would *you* like to be tortured?" A fanatical Nazi might well say in response: "I happen to think Jews are so disgusting that if I were a Jew, I too would deserve to be tortured." At this point there is little the Kantian can say to change the Nazi's mind. You can't, as the old saying goes, argue with a sick mind, and the logic underpinning Kant's theory breaks down when it comes up against murderous Nazis, suicide bombers, and other fanatics.

Kantian ethics overlooks the importance of the consequences of actions, and it also assumes that the universalizability principle can be applied *objectively* to highly subjective situations. These problems notwithstanding, Kantian ethics remains a major influence on thinking about ethics in the Western tradition. Its emphasis on the idea that we have a duty to do the right thing for its own sake appeals to many people, but perhaps even more important is its implication that there is such a thing as the right thing to do in any given circumstance. Moral choices are black and white for Kant, and moral rights and wrongs are absolute and objective. Moreover, Kant thinks that moral rights and wrongs are transparent from a rational standpoint. Kant's conviction that moral matters are clear and objective stands in stark contrast with the murkiness and complexity that typically attach to real-world moral problems—think of the abortion debate, for example—but whether Kant's confidence is warranted is something that remains a matter of intense debate.

4.5: VIRTUE ETHICS, SOCIAL CONTRACT, AND OTHER THEORIES

There are many more theories of ethics than those we have surveyed so far, indeed too many to cover in a book of this nature, but a few others deserve at least passing mention. Among these alternative approaches, two of the more important are virtue ethics and social contract theories of ethics.

Two questions form the basis of an approach to ethics dating back to Aristotle: What is the good life and how are we to achieve it? For some, the good life means owning fast cars, yachts, expensive houses, and having a lot of money. And for others, leading a happy family life, having loving relationships or pursuing a rewarding career might be the essence of a good life. But although details of what constitutes the good life may vary from one person to another, what these differing conceptions have in common is the idea of striving to realize our full potential in life. The idea of self-realization, or self-actualization, sounds as if it originated with the New Age movement, but Aristotle had already discussed it at great length.

Aristotle defined the good life in terms what he called *eudaimonia*, which loosely translates as happiness, where happiness is interpreted as being not merely pleasure, but also as living well or excellently. There are both moral and intellectual virtues, according to Aristotle, and they must be cultivated, just as a musician needs to cultivate her musical talent. Aristotle also thought that virtue is a feature of one's character, and that it is characteristic of a virtuous person that she wants to be virtuous. But what exactly *are* moral virtues? Interestingly, Aristotle thought that they are "means between the extremes" of certain characteristics. For example, courage is the mean between the extremes of cowardice and recklessness, pride falls between the extremes of humility and vanity, being charitable means being neither too generous nor too stingy, and so on. This doctrine is sometimes mistaken to mean that we should do all things in moderation, but this is not quite what Aristotle had in mind, for he thought that there cannot be too much of a good thing when it comes to virtue.

Chief among the virtues for humans is a life of intellectual activity, since exercising our rational faculties is the primary purpose of our lives and most apt to make us happy. Not one to deny himself worldly pleasures and rewards, the good life for Aristotle includes the enjoyment of good food and fine wine in moderation, as well as the pursuit of pleasure, wealth, success, involvement in civic affairs, and, above all, philosophical contemplation. While few of us would find much to object to in a life such as this, Aristotle's theory of ethics as virtuous living has little to offer us when it comes to resolving specific moral problems in the real world. What should we do about euthanasia or censorship on the Internet or the proliferation of genetically modified organisms? It is not clear that Aristotle's conception of the good life helps us sort out issues such as these, and so, while it is of considerable interest and merit in its own right, virtue ethics is perhaps too limited to serve as the basis of a general theory of ethics.

Social contract theories offer yet another perspective on ethics, and their focus is on how morals emerge in social contexts. Early proponents of this line of thinking include Thomas Hobbes (1588–1679) and John Locke (1632–1704), while among contemporary contractarian theorists, the Canadian philosopher David Gauthier (1932–) has made important contributions to the field. The premise of this cluster of theories is that ethics is a function of the typically unwritten and unspoken agreements or contracts that exist among individual members of a society and which constitute society as a whole. In as much as they attempt to explain how morality actually functions in society, social contract theories are essentially descriptive in nature, but to the extent that they seek to spell out the ideal balance between the rights of individuals and those of the community, they are also prescriptive.

According to contractarian thinkers, if no rules or laws are in place to govern the behavior of individuals, then individuals have maximum freedom. We may think of this condition of living in accordance with the law of the jungle as the *state of nature*. The disadvantage of such a state is that it leaves individuals extremely insecure and vulnerable to attack by others. The thinking goes that in forming societies, humans trade off some of their personal freedom in order to partake of the benefits of participating in society. These benefits include cooperative ventures such as education and transportation systems made possible by living in large groups, and heightened personal security, courtesy of organized public security forces. The purpose of social contract theories is to spell out equitable rules for the formation of social living arrangements. Contractarian thinking was highly influential on the founding fathers of the United States, an influence reflected in documents like the US Constitution and the Declaration of Independence. Indeed, many contemporary social and moral problems, such as property rights, gun control, smokers' rights, censorship, and so on, are directly related to the problem of balancing the rights of individuals with the rights of the community, which through its government imposes restrictions on our behavior.

While social contract thinkers believe that we need to leave nature behind before ethics can emerge, others have sought to explain ethics *in terms of* nature, and in particular human nature. On this view, to live ethically is to be mindful of what human nature is and to live in accordance with it. For some philosophers, such as Aristotle and Aquinas, human nature is fixed and preordained—in Aquinas's case by God—while for others, such as the biologist E.O. Wilson (1929–) and other sociobiologists, human nature results from the contingent processes of Darwinian evolution. There are two glaring difficulties with theories of this sort, which are called *natural law theories*. First, the very idea that there is such a thing as human nature is highly controversial in the social sciences, and secondly, even if it exists, it is by no means obvious that any number of facts about humans can or should dictate to us how we ought to behave (recall Hume's "is-ought" fallacy in § 4.1). Perhaps, as Katherine Hepburn tells Humphrey Bogart in *The African Queen*, nature is what we were put on earth to rise above.

Whereas natural law theorists take ethics to have been determined by forces or processes beyond our control, there is a tradition in Continental philosophy that sees ethics as the highly malleable creation of individuals. Friedrich Nietzsche advocated a particularly strident version of this view. Nietzsche despised the dominance of Christianity in the history of ethics in the West, which he thought of as fostering a collective attitude of servitude and submission. He challenges us to exercise our "will to power" and to construct our moral selves in the image of the *Übermensch* (or Superman). The Nazi party was drawn to Nietzsche's ideas, but Nietzsche was not himself anti-Semitic and the Nazis grossly distorted his teachings about the *Übermensch*.

A more modern movement that also assumes that we are faced with having to create ethics on an individual level is *existentialism*. Existentialists, in particular Jean-Paul Sartre and the novelist Albert Camus (1913–60), see the human condition as consisting of the continual process of making moral choices, and claim that these choices shape our lives. There is neither outside help nor moral absolutes available to guide us in our decision-making. To be human is to be condemned to be free and to be continually making moral decisions. It is our need for authenticity—our need to be true to ourselves—that ultimately guides our choices. Existentialists exerted considerable influence over European intellectuals in the decades immediately after World War II, but the influence of the movement has waned in recent years.

4.6: FEMINIST THEORY AND LOVE

The emergence of the feminist movement in the nineteenth and twentieth centuries brought with it profound challenges to the male-dominated history of ethics and philosophy in general. Early proponents of feminist thought, including J.S. Mill, who wrote *The Subjection of Women* in 1869, and Mary Wollstonecraft (1759–97), whose *A Vindication of the Rights of Woman* remains a classic in the field, focused on the rationale for extending basic rights, such as rights to education and participation in politics, to women. Suffragettes and later liberal feminists pursued these and other causes in the twentieth century, championing a host of equal rights, opportunity and compensation issues for women, struggles that sadly still have a long way to go in too much of the world. Radical feminists go further in their critiques of patriarchy, arguing for a restructuring of society to represent the interests and values of women, and in some cases even arguing for the superiority of women and their values to those of men.

In ethics, some feminist challenges are motivated by the inadequacies they allege plague traditional theories of ethics. For example, for all the differences in their respective philosophical outlooks, Mill, Kant, Aristotle, and most other male philosophers have much in common in terms of their methodologies. Specifically, such thinkers tend to assume that rationality, objectivity, the autonomy of individuals and the pursuit of abstract principles are fundamental tenets of philosophical methodology, assumptions that are questioned, if not rejected outright, by many feminists. Of more recent feminist thinkers, Genevieve Lloyd (1941–) has taken a leading role with her attack on what she calls in the title of one of her books the man of reason. In this book she takes aim at the long-standing gender bias in Western philosophy. Other feminists stress the need to factor social conditions and relations into any adequate understanding of morality, while Virginia Held (1929–), Carol Gilligan (1936–), and Nel Noddings (1929–) have all argued that theories of ethics need to take into account what they claim to be distinctively women's ways of thinking about moral issues. Some feminists promote concepts such as caring, nurturing, inclusiveness, and consensus as the hallmarks of an alternative, feminist ethics. No one, definitive, feminist conception of ethics has emerged to date, and it is quite likely that no such conception will emerge, given the plurality and range of feminist voices and concerns in ethics. In this respect, feminist ethics reflects feminist thought in general, which is a broad intellectual, social, and political movement, and is applicable to a wide range of philosophical concerns, from epistemology to literary criticism to philosophy of science to philosophy of language, and beyond.

There is little doubt about the legitimacy of the feminist criticism that male philosophers have historically either overlooked or else simply rejected those moral concerns of particular interest to women, such as the role emotions play in our moral lives. But whether there are distinctively feminine ways of thinking about ethics is a deep and controversial matter. This issue brings into play questions about whether such putative differences are essential or not, whether they are rooted in biology or in culture, and so on, all of which are important but difficult and unresolved issues. Whether claims about feminine virtues and values such as caring and nurturing comprise robust enough foundations for a genuinely alternative conception of ethics remains an open question—a question that is central to contemporary debates about the nature and status of feminist ethics.

Perhaps no discussion of how we should treat ourselves and other people is complete without at least a passing mention of the relevance of love to the search for solutions to our moral problems. Plato turned his attention to the topic of love in his timeless dialogue *The Symposium*. More recently, the Beatles informed us that all we need is love. The great British Prime Minister Benjamin Disraeli went so far as to suggest that love is the very principle of existence and its only end. Without digressing to explore the many manifestations of love, such as erotic love, filial love, and the love of beauty, I shall take it as fairly safe to say that people the world over agree that love of ourselves and each other is good, desirable, and an end in itself. Moreover, love is a powerful antidote to the enmities, hatreds, conflicts, and intolerance that exist among us. Sadly, however, while generation after generation subscribes to homilies about the power of love, love seems to have done little to mitigate these problems. Why? If it is so obvious that were humanity to avail itself of the prescription of love, moral ills would be cured, then why has this utopian state never come to pass? Why have we failed so abjectly to take our own advice?

The urge to love is unquestionably deep-seated, redeeming and, in the case of its erotic manifestation, an exquisitely pleasurable and life-affirming impulse. But although a world filled with love would lead to harmony in interpersonal relationships, perhaps our yearning for this end state fails to take into account the human condition and what animates us. Heraclitus took conflict to be a fundamental, generative metaphysical principle, and if this idea has any merit, then perhaps peace on earth is forever destined to remain a chimera. Moreover, Leibniz argued that while God could well have chosen to create a world filled with love, such a world would not have been optimal from the creator's perspective. According to Leibniz's account of the existence of evil, of which more in Chapter Six, a world ruled by love would have been less interesting, stimulating and challenging than the one which, for better or worse, we find ourselves inhabiting.

Studies in contemporary ethics have recently been given new urgency by a host of developments in the biomedical sciences and biotechnology. In the field of biomedical science, for example, new reproductive technologies have thrust into the spotlight unsettling questions about *in vitro* fertilization, the storage and fate of surplus embryos, and surrogate motherhood. The rapid unravelling of the secrets of genetics has also presented us with a new set of problems. In this case the problems have to do with the ownership, rights, and potential dangers associated with new, genetically modified organisms; the proliferation of animal, and possibly very soon human, clones; and so-called stem-cell research, with its looming promise of organisms generated for the purpose of supplying replacement organs for humans. The need for informed public debate about such issues is pressing and vital, especially given that the rapid pace of innovations in biotechnology outstrips the public's ability to digest, much less evaluate, the numerous and thorny ethical issues surrounding these advances.

4.7: CONCLUSION

This brings to a close our brief survey of theories of ethics in the Western tradition. Unfortunately, if not surprisingly, we have found that firm conclusions about specific ethical problems are exceedingly hard to come by. Nevertheless, ethical issues and our responses to them are unique in philosophy because of the magnitude of the impact they have on our day-to-day lives. What we can say is that the gravity of ethical questions is predicated on the assumption that we are genuinely free to make decisions and choices that affect ourselves and those around us. The source of the need to decide ethical issues in turn stems from our capacity to experience suffering, as well as from our capacity to empathize with the suffering of others.

That said, the underlying question remains: Do our capacities for suffering and compassion for others have any enduring significance beyond ourselves? Is anything *truly* morally good or bad, or *truly* morally right or wrong? Or are all our notions about moral right and wrong subject to change in the long term, just like so much else of human thought and culture? To pose these questions is to ask whether ethics has an objective basis. In the final chapter we return to questions of what objectivity is and what it entails.

CHAPTER 5

Science:

Space, Time, Change, and the Infinite

In terms of rational thoughts, the Absolute [infinite] is unthinkable
… real knowledge of the Absolute must be mystical, if indeed such a
thing as mystical knowledge is possible.

— RUDY RUCKER

5.0: INTRODUCTION

In this chapter, we survey some topics situated at the intersection
of philosophy, physics, and mathematics, namely: space, time,
the nature of change, and the infinite. We will frame some of the
discussion of these concepts in terms of contrasting metaphysical viewpoints. In the case of space and time, the contrast in question concerns whether these concepts are *absolute* or *relative*,
while the discussion of change focuses on whether change takes
place *discretely* or *continuously*.

  Some connections between the four concepts featured in this
chapter suggest themselves readily, whereas others are subtler and
less intuitive. For example, time and change share obvious affini-
ties, to the point that, on some accounts at least, the two are one
and the same. Likewise infinity and space, both of which seem to
be ideal exemplars of our understanding of endlessness. Our qual-

itative experience of space and time is that they are very different, but from the perspective of relativistic physics they are thoroughly entwined. Moreover, space and time share commonalities of a quite different sort in Kant's philosophy. But while all four of these concepts are of special interest to philosophers, the roles they play and the techniques used to manipulate them in the hard sciences, particularly in mathematics and physics, vary significantly. Mathematical spaces, for example, unlike the wide-open spaces of the prairies, are pure and abstract, and while time certainly does enter into some areas of mathematics, such as calculus, it appears in physics as a multi-faceted quantity, wearing different hats depending on the branch of physics under consideration.

5.1: From Space and Time to Space-time

If we are asked to describe space, notions such as emptiness, nothingness or absence are likely to spring to mind. And indeed, these notions do apply to certain conceptions of space, such as the pristine spaces of mathematics and the theory advanced by the ancient Greek Atomists, who took reality to consist of tiny, indivisible, material particles hurtling around and occasionally colliding with each other in an infinite void. But philosophers and scientists have entertained a surprisingly diverse range of theories about the nature of space, some of which preserve little of our pre-theoretic notions of space as mere emptiness or nothingness. A hallmark of a genuine philosophical problem is that no firm consensus exists regarding the true nature of the subject, and in this regard space is no exception.

What, then, *is* space? The air surrounding us provides us with plenty of elbow room, but it is a really a motley assortment of atmospheric gases, pollutants, dust, and other small particles. Indeed, in the cosmological theories of many of the ancient Greeks, air was just one among several physical substances. Outer space is more rarefied than the air found in the earth's atmosphere, but it still teems with cosmic gases, particles, and radiation. In their quest to create ideal conditions in which to perform certain experiments, physicists will sometimes pump the air out of a bell jar, which creates a vacuum, but quantum physicists tell us that elementary particles flit in and out of existence even in a perfect vacuum. This accords neatly with Spinoza's insistence that "nature abhors a vacuum," which in turn forms part of an alternative tradition—supported by Aristotle and Descartes, among others—that construes space as a *plenum*, or fullness, rather than as a form of emptiness.

It is beginning to look as though the physical phenomena we frequently identify with space turn out to be highly material in nature, only less dense than ordinary liquids and solid objects. If this is the case, however, then what has happened to space? At a naïve level, space seems to be the medium or receptacle in which objects reside and events take place. But if space is really just another physical entity, albeit a highly diffuse one, then perhaps it is really just a means by which we speak about and delineate the denser objects that are of interest to us. For example, an interior decorator might want to create more or less space between the television and the couch.

These two ways of looking at and thinking about space reflect a deeper, underlying question about whether space is absolute or relative. What I have characterized as the naïve view of space as a receptacle is associated with the idea that space is absolute, while the account that sees space as consisting in relations between objects corresponds to the theory that space is relative. Historically, the clash between these starkly different conceptions of space was articulated most vividly in a lucid but acrimonious exchange between Leibniz and Newton, or at least between Leibniz and one of Newton's followers, since the ungracious Newton would have nothing to do with Leibniz. For Newton, space is a sort of fixed, immovable setting within which the actions of physical forces and motions play themselves out upon objects. Absolute space also guarantees that there is an absolute reference frame with respect to which changes in the locations of material bodies take place. A reference frame consists of the immediate spatial surroundings within which an observer is situated and performs measurements. Newton also thought that time as measured by our more or less accurate time-keeping instruments only approximates perfectly accurate absolute time, which elapses quite independently of any measurement of it. The death knell for Newtonian absolute space came, however, with a definitive experiment in the late nineteenth century conducted by two American physicists called Michelson and Morley.

If absolute space exists, then it must be permeated by a medium through which light travels. As far back as the time of the ancient Greeks, various thinkers had theorized about the existence of this medium, also known as the "ether." If the ether exists, then the motion of the earth through the ether should create a kind of wind, similar to the wind you would experience if you were driving in a convertible on a still day with the top down. This ether wind would in turn deflect light passing through it, and the Michelson-Morley experiment was designed to detect such deflections. A positive result would have vindicated Newton, but the result was negative, and so Newtonian absolute space was decisively refuted.

Leibniz thought that in a world of empty space there would be nothing to distinguish one spatial point from another. For Leibniz, space is relative, a matter merely of how we happen to perceive things as coexisting in relation to each other, and similarly time is a matter of how we perceive succession. Assuming that there is an absolute reference frame, the contents of the world could have been shifted, say, one inch to the left; and assuming the existence of absolute time, God could presumably have created the world one hour sooner. But Leibniz thought that no adequate, or sufficient, reasons could explain such possibilities. Leibniz's relational theories of space and time accord with his *principle of sufficient reason*, which asserts that nothing exists or takes place without adequate reason. Logically speaking, this principle does not depend upon the existence of God, although Leibniz here implicitly identifies reason with the mind of a rational God. Without a rational God, however, his argument is far less compelling. The prospect of a capricious God or a world in which some things just are one way rather than another for no good reason might be unpalatable to a rationalist like Leibniz, but neither scenario is logically impossible.

As we saw in Chapter Three, a very different way of thinking about space and time, one oriented towards epistemology rather than metaphysics, comes from Immanuel Kant. For Kant, space and time are what he calls "forms of intuition," by which he means that they are integral to the way our minds are constituted. Rather than learning *from* experience that space exists outside ourselves, which realists about space such as Newton would have us believe, Kant argues instead that the outside world is a representation made possible only because our minds are structured in such a way as to make possible the perception of space. Similar considerations apply to time, which Kant thinks is not an independently existing feature of the physical world, but rather a feature of the way in which our minds structure, and indeed create the very conditions of, sensory experience. Although they are essentially subjective, Kant thought of these features of our psyches as nevertheless fixed and unalterable, somewhat surprisingly rejecting the relational theory of space in favour of the absolute view. In defense of this position, he asks us to consider a universe devoid of everything except a single human hand. The relations between the points on the fingers and palm of the hand are the same with respect to each other, regardless of whether it is a left or a right hand. But these relations alone do not determine whether the imaginary limb is a left or a right hand, which are incongruent mirror images of each other and thus objectively different from each other.

Kant lumps space and time together as forms of intuition, but time seems to raise some unique puzzles and problems. For his part, Kant articulates the difference between space and time by claiming that, whereas space is a matter of the representation of "outer experience," the relations of time make possible the "intuition of inner states" as well. Whether or not this distinction between inner states and outer experience captures the difference between space and time accurately, Kant rightly notes that our experiences of space and time are qualitatively very different. Unlike space, which seems to be out there as an all-encompassing, monolithic presence, time gives the impression of flowing past us like some vast, interminable, and ever-changing river. The temporal concepts of past, present, and future are asymmetrical in a way that the directions of space are not, and time's duration seems to be qualitatively different from the expanse of space. True, we do say that we move through space as well as through time, but the experience of time as flowing appears to distinguish it from the static nature of spatial concepts such as position and location.

When we pause to reflect on the brevity of life and our looming mortality, nothing seems more real than the passage of time, but what do we mean when we refer to the *passage* or *flow* of time? We measure flow rates of liquids or gases in terms of volume per unit of time, but as the philosopher J.J.C. Smart (1920–) pointedly asked: How fast does time flow? To answer that it flows at a rate of one second per second gets us nowhere, nor does the suggestion that there must be a master clock somewhere in the universe that keeps proper track of time, for what reason would we have to think that *that* clock measures the "real" passage of time? Puzzles of this sort have led philosophers such as Smart and others to dismiss the idea of time-flow as an illusion. But however intellectually compelling such arguments might be, it is difficult to imagine that time does anything *but* pass, and in this sense Kant might be right after all. It's little wonder that St. Augustine (354–430) was driven to remark that time is something he understands perfectly well until he tries to explain it.

As different as space and time appear to be at an intuitive level, Albert Einstein (1879–1955) unified them in his groundbreaking theories of special and general relativity. Of his many deep insights, perhaps Einstein's greatest was the idea of combining the principle that motion is relative, which had also been upheld by Galileo and Ernst Mach, with the idea that the speed of light in a vacuum is constant and universal, regardless of one's frame of reference. This means that the velocity of a beam of light as measured by any observer is the same, irrespective of the speed or direction of motion of the observer. The only way Einstein could consistently integrate these two principles, however, was to give up on the Newtonian idea that space and time are absolute.

Some startling consequences follow from these deceptively simple precepts. Time suddenly becomes a dimension best understood as a form of distance. These days we speak of the distance light travels in a year relative to any observer as a *light-year*. And three-dimensional space for an observer may be thought of as a relationship that holds between events that are temporally simultaneous. Moreover, space and time are elastic in Einstein's world, whereas the speed of light remains constant. Another mind-boggling consequence of this revolutionary theory is the phenomenon of *time dilation*. What this means is that two clocks in motion relative to each other do not measure time as elapsing at the same rate, although the experience of time passing is exactly the same for the observers in the same reference frames as the clocks they accompany. Discrepancies regarding elapsed time recorded by their clocks arise only when the observers compare their clock readings. This has been well confirmed in experiments using atomic clocks. Observers are affected by relative motion in the sense that the faster that person *A* travels with respect to the frame of reference of person *B*, the slower *A* will age with respect to *B*, even though *A* does not detect anything abnormal about the rate at which she ages.

The strange consequences of Einstein's theories of relativity are too complex and numerous to delve into in any great detail here, but one consequence, the so-called *relativity of simultaneity*, is worth mentioning. If time differences are relative to the motions of observers, then what counts as the present, past, and future for person *A* will be different for person *B* who is in motion with respect to *A*. More specifically, an event which is in *A*'s future—or more correctly, in the future light-cone of *A*—might well be in *B*'s past! The Newtonian paradigm of absolute space and time has given way to a radically different model consisting of events populating a space-time manifold, where past, present, and future are conceived of as events co-existing at different locations. In the theory of general relativity, separation is no longer solely a spatial concept, but also a temporal one, and space-time is a kind of four-dimensional fabric that folds, warps, and stretches in the presence of massive objects such as a sun, planet or galaxy. This last point raises the intriguing possibility that we may one day be able to manipulate this fabric in such a way as to traverse temporally distant regions instantaneously, thereby perhaps even meeting up with past or future versions of ourselves in the process. Philosophers and scientists continue to debate such problems and their implications.

This highly simplified and condensed introduction to Einstein's thought glosses over many important concepts and distinctions, such as the difference between uniform and accelerated motion, and it also neglects the contributions of Lorentz, Minkowski, and other physicists in the development of Einstein's thought. A thorough appreciation of Einstein's theories of relativity and his other contributions to the history of ideas requires a much deeper study of mathematics and physics than we can undertake here.

5.2 : Some Ancient Greek Ideas about Change

It goes without saying that change is an all-pervasive aspect of reality and the human condition. But what exactly *is* change and what are its characteristics? Does it occur smoothly and continuously, or is it discrete and jumpy in nature, like the movements of dancers under a strobe light at a disco? The best efforts of physicists, mathematicians, and philosophers to answer these questions have so far yielded a tantalizing mixture of insight and the kind of frustration St. Augustine experienced in his struggle to define time. Of course, this similarity is hardly coincidental, since the concepts of time and change are so closely interconnected. To begin our survey of ideas about change, let us revisit some of the theories we touched on in Chapter One about the nature of change and reality.

For two diametrically opposing metaphysical positions regarding change, we return, as we often do in metaphysics, to the Pre-Socratics. The two extremes to which I refer are these: nothing really changes at all, and everything is constantly in a state of change. Parmenides advocated the former theory, while Heraclitus defended the latter. We briefly discussed Parmenides, Heraclitus, and Zeno in Chapter One, but it is worth revisiting the ideas of these seminal figures in Western thought in slightly more detail, bearing in mind the usual caveat that applies to the Pre-Socratics, which is that our knowledge of their theories is fragmentary at best.

For Parmenides, reality is eternal, fixed, and unchanging. Of course, at the level of everyday experience, change abounds, but if we were able to apprehend reality as a whole, we would understand the experience of change as a function of our limited perspectives of reality. To help us better appreciate what Parmenides might have been getting at, consider the following metaphysical picture of the world. Think of reality as one big movie. If you're a theist, you might think of God as being the producer and director of the film. Now imagine unraveling the huge roll of the film of reality and viewing it by rushing past it at high speed. What you would perceive as you move past the frames would be the appearance of motion and change in the film. But considering the roll of film as a whole, no change or motion really takes place at all; it is just a big roll of film consisting of frames that comprise every event that has ever occurred. Of course, this is similar to what occurs when we watch an ordinary movie in a cinema, except that there the film itself is moved through a projector, and the appearance of motion and change occurs on the screen.

Parmenides's disciple Zeno concocted a series of brilliant paradoxes to demonstrate his master's teachings about the unreality of time, motion, and change. One of them, known as the Arrow, is comparable to the thought experiment we have just entertained. Consider an arrow in flight. Does it move? Zeno argues that at every instant of its flight, the arrow is at some fixed, spatial location, and that at each of these instants the arrow is motionless. But the trajectory of the arrow in flight surely consists of nothing more than a collection of these instants, none of which is actually moving. Where has the motion of the arrow gone? It would seem that movement somehow has to take place *between* these instants, but how is this possible?

A variation of another of Zeno's paradoxes, which we sketched in Chapter One, implies not only that I cannot even get from here to the door of this room, but that I do not move at all! The upshot of the argument is that in order for me to get to the door, I would have to perform an infinite number of movements, but for Zeno it is logically impossible to do this in any finite period of time, no matter how quickly I perform these movements. Either it takes me an infinitely long period of time to get to the door, which renders motion effectively impossible, or else I cannot change my position in any finite period of time, in which case motion is also effectively impossible. Zeno's arguments have fascinated philosophers and mathematicians ever since their inception, and mathematicians have devised ever more sophisticated techniques to refute them. We will return to a standard mathematical refutation of Zeno's paradoxes later.

Some of the most famous metaphysical descendants of Parmenides include Spinoza and Einstein, both of whom envisage the world as a kind of vast, deterministic system in which all past, present, and future events co-exist. This yields a metaphysical structure that we might call a "block universe," because on this account one takes the universe to be one big, self-contained blob or block made up of all of the constituents of reality. As we saw in the previous section, for Einstein the fabric of this block is the geometry of space-time, in which is embedded the spatio-temporal events of reality. On this view, each of our lives may be thought of as a unique string of space-time events. A slightly more technical term for one of these threads in Einstein's block universe is a *world-line*. A world-line, then, is analogous to a segment of the film of reality we discussed earlier, except that for Einstein, reality has more dimensions than an ordinary, two-dimensional filmstrip.

Parmenides's sophisticated but profoundly counter-intuitive metaphysical system cast a long shadow over his successors in the ancient world, and some of the most important writings of both Plato and Aristotle were devoted to reconciling how it is that some things can somehow remain the same in what is so obviously an ever-changing world. This is not the place to enter into a detailed discussion of either Plato or Aristotle, but it is worth noting that Plato, like Parmenides, exhibited a deep antipathy toward, and distrust of, the idea of basing absolute truths and knowledge on the shifting sands of the world of everyday experience.

At the other end of the spectrum from Parmenides was Heraclitus. The writings of Heraclitus were regarded as notoriously cryptic and obscure even in his own time, but his basic teaching was that everything is in a state of ceaseless change or flux. This doctrine is encapsulated in the famous adage: *You cannot step into the same river twice*, the reason being that a river is constantly flowing and therefore never the same from one moment to the next. How does the Heraclitean view of change as a kind of fundamental metaphysical principle fare in comparison with Parmenides? Heraclitus seems to present a reasonable and defensible position, but it, too, is beset with a variety of problems. First, taking change to be a fundamental metaphysical principle forces us to accept the paradoxical view that change is a constant. Is the principle of change itself subject to change? If so, then it cannot be a fundamental metaphysical principle after all, but if not, then it appears that there is something that doesn't change after all. In fairness to Heraclitus, we should add that he also believed in the existence of a rational principle called *logos*, which apparently transcends the ceaseless swirl of change, but whether, and if so how, he reconciled *logos* and change is unclear.

5.3: CRATYLUS, ARISTOTLE, AND THE IDENTITY CRISIS OF HERACLITUS

Cratylus pointed out that Heraclitus runs into a nasty problem of determinacy and identity. The problem is this: Heraclitus would have us believe that we cannot step into the same river twice, but if, as Heraclitus claims, everything really is constantly changing, how can a fixed, determinate entity such as a river exist in the first place? Cratylus effectively pointed out that if stepping into "the same" river a second time presents a problem, then we are forced to question the existence of the river the first time around. What Cratylus was getting at is that in a world of ceaseless change, the existence of objects at some point *in* time is as problematic as their existence *over* time. How is it that an object can exist at some point in time if it has no fixed, determinate existence over time? Logically, I see nothing that rules out an ontology of instantaneously existing objects. In such a world, nothing exists for more than an instant, but this view is so extreme as to be just as counter-intuitive as the metaphysics of Parmenides. We routinely refer to people, places, and things as if they are in some sense the same objects they were a second, an hour, a day, or even a century ago, but in a world comprising nothing but instantaneously existing objects, such talk would be nonsense.

Both of the above theories of change lead to highly counter-intuitive conclusions. Is a compromise between these two implausible extremes possible? One influential attempt to resolve this dilemma comes to us from Aristotle. Aristotle sought to explain how objects could change over time and yet still retain their identity. Aristotle's theory is based on distinguishing between an object's *essential* properties and its *accidental* properties. "Essential" in this context means intrinsic or inherent, whereas "accidental" means incidental or contingent. An object typically has both kinds of properties, according to Aristotle. For example, it is an essential property of me that I am a human being, but an accidental property that I happen to have no beard. The difference between these properties is that I could grow a beard in the future without altering my identity, but I cannot, for example, shed the property of being a human without losing my identity. On this account, then, it makes sense to imagine me as say, once having been younger, or shorter, or bald, or even as being in Mexico right now instead of Calgary, but it is nonsense to try to imagine me as a banana, or a table, or a cup of coffee. The former changes are only changes of my accidental properties, whereas changes of the latter sort would mean that I would no longer be me.

Aristotle's theory is subtle, complex, and debated vigorously to this day, but it has the virtue, on the face of it at least, of conforming to common sense, a feature all too rare in metaphysical theories. After all, you would surely agree that the you who is reading this book is, in an important and intuitively obvious sense, the same you who opened the book before starting to read it, the same you as the person you remember having acquired the book, having long ago learned to read, and so on. Things like changes in your location, the gain or loss of a few pounds every now and then, to changes in your attitudes about certain subjects do, of course, signify changes, even important ones, but the point is that you—and the rest of us—recognize them as changes happening to you *yourself*, not changes of you into something completely new and different. Whatever other merits Aristotle's theory might have, it succeeds in drawing our attention to differences in the *kinds* of changes an entity might undergo. Two such changes, changes of position and changes of composition, are what we discuss next.

As we have already seen, a change of position as it pertains to something like a person does not necessarily affect that thing's basic identity. That is to say, I don't change into something entirely different by leaving the room I'm in. But changes in composition are a different matter. If I gain or lose a few pounds over the years, most people would agree that my identity remains unaffected. There could be fatter or thinner versions of me, but those versions are still essentially me. But what if surgical techniques advance to the point where we are able to perform successful brain transplants, and suppose I have a brain exchange operation with you? When my body wakes up after the anesthetic wears off, would you be inhabiting my body while I discover what it's like to have your body, or would I have the sensation of feeling a little strange at first with a different brain in my head but gradually get used to the new organ, just as I would get used to any other new organ or prosthetic device after a more conventional surgery? Does my identity go with my brain or my body? Or does it somehow go with a combination of both? If the latter, would the operations leave both of us confused about our identities? Of course the exact same questions also arise for you. I will leave these questions for you to ponder.

A related problem is a puzzle called *the ship of Theseus*. The ship of the Greek hero Theseus is kept afloat over the years by replacing its parts one by one. Suppose that the individual planks, mast, sails, and even the nameplate are all replaced until not one of the original components remains. Now suppose that years later someone reassembles the *Theseus* using only the original components. Which is the *real Theseus*, the one we kept calling the *Theseus* over the years, or the newly re-constructed original? There are conflicting intuitions here, but no clear answers. The relevance of this puzzle to the subject of change and personal identity is that, like the *Theseus*, our bodies are in a constant state of repair. At the cellular level, we repair, renew, and replace parts of ourselves all the time, which is one reason we need to eat as much as we do. Cell components such as cell walls, intra-cellular fluids, proteins, and so on are in need of continuous regeneration. In fact, over the course of about seven years, every one of our atoms and molecules is replaced. This means that on a purely physical level you are a totally different person from the one you were seven years ago! However, we have no difficulty recognizing ourselves as being the same for much longer periods of time than that, and from a legal perspective we remain the same persons throughout our lives.

One explanation of how we manage to perform this feat of recognition goes something like this. We do not identify a person in terms of her constituent atoms, molecules or chemicals, but rather in terms of her overall *form*. The atoms in a strand of DNA might all be replaced, but the overall structure or form of the DNA can remain unchanged. What is interesting about this explanation, however, is that forms, patterns, and structures are not, strictly speaking, purely physical or material in nature, but rather conceptual. But if our understanding of identity involves conceptual, as opposed to purely physical, elements, this constitutes an argument against the view that our existence is solely physical or material in nature. Once again, a consideration of problems of change and identity leads us into deep metaphysical waters.

5.4: CHANGE IN MATHEMATICS AND PHYSICS

Next, let us turn to how the notion of change is handled in mathematics and physics. The history of mathematics in Western thought is the story of two venerable traditions: the *arithmetic* and the *geometric*. Arithmetic is rooted in our tendency to break up the world into parts, quantify things and count them, while geometry is a function of our urge to organize the world in terms of spatial structure and order. Of course, both branches of mathematics have important practical applications, but these need not detain us here. Arithmetic is the domain of numbers and numerical operations, which are *discrete* in nature, whereas geometry deals with lines, curves, areas, and volumes, which are *continuous* concepts. The interplay between the notions of the discrete and the continuous has been responsible for a particularly productive and creative tension in mathematics and physics. Calculus, modern theories of infinity and quantum physics are just some of the fields in which problems of reconciling the discrete and the continuous arise, but we do not have to study these subjects to appreciate why the discrete and the continuous are so difficult to unify.

I said earlier that geometry deals with continuous concepts, but that's not exactly right. Geometry also includes the concept of a point. From a geometrical perspective, a line is made up of many points, none of which are spatially extended. Moreover, mathematicians tell us that lines have a property called denseness, meaning that between any two points, no matter how close together they are, you can always fit another one. How can many things, none of which are spatially extended, form something that is spatially extended? On the one hand, movement along a line is continuous and lines are smooth, not gappy. After all, if you were dangling from the end of a rope and the rope had gaps in it, you'd fall to the ground, right? This seems very simple. We represent points, which are geometrical concepts, with numbers, which are isolated and discrete things. The numbers we use to represent points on a line have infinite decimal expansions and are called *real* numbers, but for practical purposes we always round off real numbers in order to perform calculations with them. Now I can easily imagine moving along a line, but how do I get from one number to another? Normally, I get from one place to another by traversing the space between them. But in the case of two consecutive numbers, such as 53 and 54, it doesn't seem to make sense to talk about the space between them, or of the space between *any* two whole numbers, for that matter. That's the problem. An interesting approach to this problem was taken by the mathematician Richard Dedekind (1831–1916), who theorized that real numbers are actually *cuts* or *gaps* situated at the interface between sets of rational numbers on a line, a theory which strangely enough ends up defining the continuity of a line in terms of a collection of gaps. This just goes to show what strange lengths mathematicians must resort to in order to reconcile the discrete and the continuous. Georg Cantor (1845–1918) devised groundbreaking theories of infinite sets and transfinite numbers that go some way towards shedding light on these problems, but they raise some difficulties of their own, as we shall see in the next section.

What has all this got to do with change, especially change in the real world? This is where physics, which is supposed to explain real-world phenomena, enters the picture. Remember Zeno's problem of motion—or rather, the problem of its impossibility? After

Newton and Leibniz introduced calculus, physicists resolved this dilemma by maintaining that bodies in motion have *instantaneous velocity*. In calculus, a moving object is assigned a velocity *and* a precise location at all times. Mathematicians pull off this trick by making use of what Newton called a fluxion, which is a ratio of a tiny bit of distance divided by a tiny bit of time, or *ds/dt* in symbolic form. What Newton and Leibniz did was to replace Zeno's frozen instants, which prohibit motion, with a series of tiny, non-zero ratios. For Berkeley, this mathematical sleight of hand was too much to swallow, and he had an excellent point, but for better or worse calculus remains at the heart of modern mathematics and physics.

While calculus is an invaluable tool for describing motion in smooth, continuous terms, it is ill suited to deal with the bizarre behavior of particles at the atomic and subatomic levels, where motion is indeterministic and jumpy. According to quantum mechanics, the area of physics that describes these particles, pairs of physical quantities such as position and momentum are such that a change in one multiplied by a change in the other is never less than a certain factor, called Planck's constant. This is the famous *uncertainty principle*. Expressed another way, the uncertainty principle means that change in quantum mechanics is discrete, or jumpy, and the factor that governs this jumpiness is Planck's constant. In quantum mechanics, change, or action, is discrete, not smooth and continuous, and the structure of quantum particles is ruled by an important set of whole numbers called quantum numbers. In the battle between the discrete and the continuous, quantum mechanics has seen the discrete take the upper hand, but whether this theory represents the last word on the subject remains to be seen.

5.5: Infinity: A Brief History

Of all the realms we explore in our philosophical travels, perhaps none is more maddening, mind-boggling, and intimidating than infinity. Situated at the intersection of mathematics, metaphysics,

physics, and theology, infinity has inspired feelings of awe, humility, bewilderment, and even outright abhorrence in those who have been courageous or foolhardy enough to enter its realm. In this section we look at some conclusions various mathematicians and philosophers have arrived at in their struggles to tame the infinite. Although most of the discussion that follows will be general and metaphysical in nature, we cannot hope to do justice to the subject without also delving into a little mathematics, which of all fields of human inquiry is most justified in calling itself the science of the infinite.

As we saw in Chapter One, the conception of the cosmos as infinite dates back at least as far as Anaximander and his theory that everything springs from the *apeiron*, the formless, chaotic, and boundless first principle of reality. The fact that the *apeiron* is disorderly reflects the trepidation that some of the ancients, including Aristotle, harbored toward the infinite. Like many fears, fears of the infinite stems from ignorance, but as confidence in our ability to unlock secrets about the extent and nature of the universe has grown, the prospect of cosmic infinitude has gradually become less daunting.

As a first step to getting a better grip on the infinite, we should note that there is a difference between infinity and endlessness. If we travel around the world, we never get to the end of the world, no matter how long or far we travel, but the earth is not infinite in extent. This is different from, say, standing on an imaginary line that stretches out in opposite directions without limit. Such a line would be infinite. The technical term in mathematics for endless but not infinite is *unbounded*, and the concept of boundedness is important in cosmology. Suppose we set out from the earth in a rocketship in an attempt to reach the outer edge of the universe. We can imagine setting our course in a straight line—strictly speaking a geodesic—in order to avoid unintentionally going around in a big circle. What is our destination likely to be? No one really knows the answer, but one thing we shouldn't expect to come across is a sign or barrier announcing the end of the universe. Any such barrier would seem to imply that something must lie beyond the barrier, or else that the barrier itself is infinitely thick. In either case the universe would have to extend beyond the point that purportedly marks its end.

Given this, what other possibilities are open regarding our quest to probe the spatial extent of the universe? One possibility is that we would journey on forever and ever without ever retracing our steps. Alternatively, we might find that, despite our best efforts to avert it, we would end up eventually retracing or intersecting our path, just as eventually happens to anyone who keeps travelling around the earth long enough. These two possibilities are respectively called "open" and "closed" universes, and which kind we happen to live in depends very much on the geometry of space-time. If space is finite but unbounded like the surface of the earth, we would sooner or later find ourselves returning to somewhere we have already been, but if space is infinite in extent, we would keep drifting further away from the earth indefinitely, never once criss-crossing our path.

This latter case is not too much more difficult to grasp than trying to imagine an infinitely long line, but there is a problem with the idea of a spatially finite and unbounded universe. We have been comparing this kind of universe to the surface of the earth, but the analogy is somewhat simplistic. In the scenario we have conjured up, the universe is a higher-dimensional sphere called a *hypersphere*. The earth is embedded in the space that surrounds it and extends beyond the solar system, but what, if anything, could the universe be floating in? There are two responses to this. One is simply to call a halt to this line of questioning altogether and insist that, as Aristotle put it, "what is limited, is not limited in reference to something that surrounds it." That is to say, Aristotle rejected as meaningless talk about what is "beyond" such a universe. The other response is to take the analogy of the earth floating in its surrounding space seriously and consistently, in which case the universe as a whole would be embedded in some even higher-dimensional medium. But far from settling matters, this move only invites new questions. Is this higher-dimensional medium infinite in extent or is it finite and unbounded? No one knows, of course, but what this shows is that, at least in the realm of cosmology, the dragon of infinity is by no means easy to slay. Coming to appreciate some of the conundrums of spatial infinity helps us understand why some philosophers, most notably Aristotle and, as we shall see in § 6.4, Aquinas after him, refuse to acknowledge that physical infinities exist, according such infinities the status of potential existence only. Interestingly enough, Aquinas believed in the existence of an infinite God possessing unlimited power, but he nevertheless thought that God "still cannot make an absolutely unlimited thing, no more than he can make an unmade thing (for this involves contradictories being true together)."

A host of cosmological problems related to the infinite also arise with respect to time. Does time have a beginning or an end? Has the universe always existed? Will it continue to exist forever? If there was a beginning of time, can it possibly make sense to ask what came before this? According to the once-popular *steady state* theory of cosmology, the universe is spatially as well as temporally infinite and is therefore conjectured always to have existed. However, this theory has been superseded in recent decades by the *big bang* theory, based on strengthening evidence that the visible universe is in the process of expanding and is roughly 10–15 billion years old. If this theory is true, then the current age of the universe is finite and space and time simultaneously came into existence with the big bang. Due to quantum effects, the big bang may have been smeared out rather than precise and instantaneous. Although at first it seems perfectly meaningful to wonder what happened before the big bang, the theory itself seems to rule out this question as meaningless on the grounds that there was no time, and therefore no events or happenings, to ask about "before" the big bang. As St. Augustine put it, the world was created *with* time, not *in* time.

Similar questions and problems also apply to the temporal end of the universe, and, as with space, answers to questions about the eventual fate of our universe rest heavily on the geometry of space-time. If the universe is open, time will be everlasting, whereas if we inhabit a closed universe, it will not go on forever. Cosmologists speculate that in a closed universe, the current process of expansion will eventually reverse itself and lead to a contracting phase, culminating in a cataclysmic final event called the *big crunch*. What would happen after the big crunch? Again, no one knows for sure, but one possibility is that the cycle of expansions and contractions we are speculating about would continue indefinitely. In this case, time would again be infinite. Yet another possibility is that in this endless cycle of oscillations, the universe might occasionally return to exactly the same state as in a previous cycle, in which case time would be circular. It might be that in the really big picture, what goes around truly does come around. Nietzsche had already entertained this *doctrine of eternal recurrence* long before the advent of modern big bang cosmology. There is something bleak and futile about the prospect of eternal recurrence, with its implication that we are but prisoners on an enormous treadmill of time, doomed to repeat history forever like the hapless protagonist in the myth of Sisyphus. On the other hand, eternal recurrence seems intuitively easier to comprehend than the idea that time comes to an end altogether in a closed universe with the coming of a big crunch.

Let us now turn from spatial and temporal infinities to mathematical notions of infinity. Numbers were probably first devised as a means of counting objects that were literally near at hand, and it is probably no coincidence that counting systems in many cultures are based on ten, the number of fingers we normally have. But tapping the real power of numbers and mathematical operations only came about when it occurred to our ancestors that the principle of counting collections of concrete objects could be abstracted and extended indefinitely. That crucial insight yielded the series of positive natural numbers: 1, 2, 3, ...; and those unassuming dots after the last numeral put us on the road to infinity. But along with the idea of unending series of numbers comes a paradox, as the great astronomer Galileo Galilei (1564–1642) noticed. This problem is seen when we compare the following two sequences, which demonstrate Galileo's paradox:

1	2	3	4	5	6	7	8	...
↕	↕	↕	↕	↕	↕	↕	↕	
10	20	30	40	50	60	70	80	...

Common sense suggests that there should be ten times as many natural numbers as there are multiples of ten shown on the bottom line. But as the arrows indicate, each of the elements in the top sequence can be matched with an element in the bottom sequence in a one-to-one manner, and this matching can be extended indefinitely. This led Galileo to conclude that "the attributes 'equal,' 'greater,' and 'less,' are not applicable to infinite, but only to finite quantities," although neither he nor anyone else was able to explain why this is so.

Another paradox of infinity, this one taken from geometry, is illustrated with the help of concentric circles. Each of the two circles in Figure 2 below comprises infinitely many points, yet every radius that extends to the outer circle intersects the inner circle at exactly one point. Consideration of this fact reveals the existence of another one-to-one correspondence, this time between the number of points on the inner circle and the number of points on the outer circle, although common sense suggests that there should be many more points on the outer circle than on the inner one.

Great strides were made in other areas of mathematics in the centuries following Galileo, but substantial progress in number theory and solving the paradoxes of infinity had to wait for the arrival of Georg Cantor. A committed advocate of the infinite, Cantor made groundbreaking contributions to areas of mathematics such as set theory and analysis. In the process of this work, Cantor revealed not only that there is an enormous multitude of infinite sets, but he also proved the remarkable result that

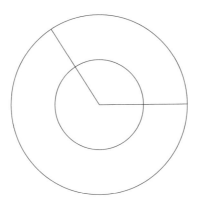

FIGURE 2

some infinities are greater than others. This ingenious proof relies on a technique called *diagonalization*, which is the same technique we used in § 3.6 to prove that not all knowledge expressible in language is knowable.

The proof that there are different orders of infinity rests on Cantor's demonstration that there is a basic distinction between countable and uncountable sets. In order to appreciate this distinction, we need to understand that numbers answer to more than one job description. Numbers can represent placeholders for ordering groups of objects, but they can also be used to indicate the sizes of collections. A bunch of 50 grapes is bigger than a bunch of 11 grapes in terms of the number of grapes, but the size of the 50th person in a line of people has nothing to do with the size of the 11th person in the line. In this context the numbers 50 and 11 are being used simply as place-holders to assign an order to the people in the line. Numbers used for ordering purposes are called *ordinals*, and numbers used to denote size are *cardinals*.

The branch of mathematics used to describe the properties of collections of objects is set theory. Just as collections come in various sizes, so too do sets. Here are two examples of finite sets: {cat, dog, mouse} and {25, 17, 3, 109, 8} (the curly braces denote sets). The set of all natural numbers, or N, is an infinite set which can be written like this: $\{0, 1, 2, 3, ...\}$. Although the set N is infinite, Cantor argues that it is countable, in the sense that each member in the set can be reached sooner or later by the methodical but reliable procedure of counting the members one by one, and he invented the cardinal number $\aleph_0$ (pronounced *aleph-null*) to denote the size of this infinite set and other infinite sets of the same size. Cantor also proved an important theorem to the effect that the set of subsets of a given set has more members than the original set. Here is an example of a set of subsets of the natural numbers consisting of just three subsets: $\{\{41, 6\}, \{2, 9, 67\}, \{1002, 983, 52, 281\}\}$. Now what about the size of the set of *all* subsets of the natural numbers? According to the theorem we just mentioned, it must have more members than the set N itself and hence be larger than $\aleph_0$. It is; in fact, Cantor proved that the set of all subsets of N—that is, the power set of N—is $2^{\aleph_0}$, which incidentally also turns out to be the cardinality of the number of points on a line and of the number of points in three-dimensional mathematical space.

Cantor introduced exotic new objects called transfinite numbers into number theory, bringing into view vast new horizons in the realm of infinity, although more conservative mathematicians initially recoiled from Cantor's playground as a mathematical chamber of horrors rather than as the paradise he envisioned. If nothing else, however, Cantor's work had a liberating effect on number theorists. Since his time even infinitesimals, infinitely small numbers that mathematicians had long ruled to be illegitimate, have attracted newfound interest. Cantor was deeply religious, and he believed that beyond the farthest reaches of the infinite cardinals lies the Absolute Infinite, or Ω. Strictly speaking, however, the Absolute Infinite is inconceivable and inaccessible to us. Indeed, the Absolute Infinite is subject to the *Reflection Principle*, which means it has the property that whatever thoughts we conjure up in our efforts to grasp the Absolute Infinite fall short of it. Even thoughts such as: *I understand that there is nothing greater than the Absolute Infinite,* or *The Absolute Infinite is what is totally inconceivable,* fail to get at it. At this point, we leave the rationality of mathematics and philosophy behind and enter the domain of faith, mysticism, and transcendence. It is fitting, then, that the topic to which we turn next is the philosophy of religion.

CHAPTER 6

Religion:
God, Evil, and the Meanings of Life

If cattle or lions had hands, so as to paint with their hands and
produce works of art as men do, they would paint their gods and
give them bodies in form like their own—horses like horses, cattle
like cattle.

— XENOPHANES

6.0: INTRODUCTION

As we saw in the introductory chapter, defining philosophy is
anything but easy or straightforward. Much the same can be said
about religion. The institutional trappings and manifestations of
religions are familiar and include churches, temples, religious
schools, ministers, rabbis, commandments, scriptures, Papal
encyclicals, and so on. Polls reveal that many people disavow alle-
giance to any established religions, yet when asked, many of these
same people insist that they are nevertheless religious. To confuse
matters further, religious language is redolent of concepts such as
God, spirituality, mystical experience, transcendence, angels, and
faith, concepts that some people profess to understand implicitly,
others have difficulty grasping, and others reject outright as
nonsensical. These confusions should alert us to the difficulties

inherent in analyzing religious concepts and language in philosophical terms.

This is not the place to undertake a survey of world religions, nor the interrelationships between religion, psychology, and society, nor alternative traditions such as Japanese Shintoism and the Dreamtime of Australia's aborigines. Our focus on Western philosophy suggests that we should confine ourselves to a consideration of the Western religious tradition alone, and even then to a limited range of issues within that tradition. Specifically, we will look at some topics at the intersection of philosophy and religion, including some forms of theism, religious belief and faith as they pertain to the concept of God, arguments for the existence of God, the problem of evil, some critiques of religion, and finally issues surrounding the meaning and purpose of life.

At the heart of both philosophy and religion is the impossibly audacious attempt to explain the nature of existence and our place in it. But religions also typically function at many other levels in society. They are often major sources of a society's cultural heritage, celebrations, holidays, collective wisdom, moral codes, rites of passage, education, ancient traditions, taboos, and customs. In addition, religions may provide guidance or options relating to a wide range of practical matters, from career choices to diets. Besides lacking this diversity of practical aspects and their overt social manifestations, philosophy differs most markedly from religion in its methods.

As we noted in the opening chapter, the practice of philosophy trades heavily on critical thinking, argumentation, dialogue, and above all on a willingness to keep an open mind about whatever topic is under consideration. Religious teachings, on the other hand, are usually based on dogma, received wisdom, beliefs or scriptures that are transmitted from person to person, and from generation to generation, in order to keep those teachings intact. Of course, oral traditions leave room for occasional embellishments, scriptures are sometimes revised or updated, and from time to time the Vatican has even changed its position or developed new policies, for example in response to challenges presented by new medical technologies. But major changes to religious doctrines tend to be the exception rather than the rule, and often come about in a bid by churches to retain their public appeal in the face of changing social attitudes. The very word "dogma," which refers specifically to a doctrine or tenet espoused by the church, is anathema to philosophers. But it is in their fundamental metaphysical concerns that philosophy and religion coincide, and it is to issues such as these we turn next.

6.1: Reason and Faith: Some Routes to Belief in God

There is far more to the philosophy of religion than questions about the existence of God, especially if we broaden our perspective and consider religious traditions worldwide; but certainly throughout the history of Western thought, the preoccupations of philosophy and religion are intertwined most intimately when it comes to *theology*, which deals with questions related to the existence of God. There are several reasons for this coincidence, some of which are historical and intellectual. Perhaps first and foremost among these reasons is the fact that, although notions of godhead and divine beings are found in many religions, all three major Western religions—Judaism, Christianity, and Islam—are *monotheistic*, meaning that they subscribe to the doctrine that there is only one God. This one God is characterized and worshipped differently in all three religions, but each has its roots in the Abraham of the Old Testament. Incidentally, these so-called Western religions originated in the Middle East, and the fact that they developed within very close geographical proximity of each other goes a long way toward explaining why the hatreds, rivalries, and jealousies that still haunt that troubled part of the world are so fierce. The philosophical roots of monotheism can in turn be traced back at least as far as the writings of Plato.

The historical influence of the church on European thinkers and philosophers can hardly be underestimated. This influence was most pronounced during the time span between the fall of the Roman Empire and the early modern period of philosophy beginning with Descartes in the seventeenth century. Throughout this period, but especially during the Middle Ages, the Church was the foremost repository of learning, education, and intellectual activity, much of which was confined to European monasteries. In addition, the Church wielded so much political and social power that serious intellectual opposition to it was not only dangerous, but for all intents and purposes out of the question. On the other hand, philosophical activity of the highest order, focused primarily on philosophical theology and logic, flourished in some of the monasteries and universities of the day. We shall shortly take a glimpse at the ideas of two of the most important figures of the time, St. Anselm (1033–1109) and St. Thomas Aquinas (1225–74), but these philosophers represent but a small sample of the many outstanding thinkers of the medieval period.

As mentioned above, the monotheism of Islam, Judaism, and Christianity is an integral part, not only of Western religious thought, but of its philosophical tradition as well. The idea that an omnipotent (or all-powerful), intelligent entity created the world is, to say the least, serviceable and in many ways a highly satisfactory solution to a host of metaphysical puzzles about the origins of, and reasons for, the existence of the cosmos. This is not to say that a belief in such an entity is correct, but rather that belief in God is attractive to some philosophers as well as adherents of certain religions. However, the basic difference between philosophers and religious believers in understanding the nature of belief in God is that for philosophers, such belief always remains tentative, speculative, and open to question, whereas for believers, God's existence is an incontrovertible fact. To put it another way, philosophers view theology in a critical light, whereas believers take the existence of God as a given and pursue theology as a means of enriching their understanding of God. In order to keep the discussion manageable, I will from here on use the word "God" to mean the God of Christianity and follow the convention of using capitalized pronouns such as "He" and "Him" for God.

Believers in the existence of God avail themselves of a number of different approaches to justifying their conviction that God exists. Broadly speaking, these justifications fall into two categories: those that make use of appeals to reason, and those that do not. Several types of explanation can be identified within each of these categories. We will identify some of these types in the remainder of this section and then discuss specific examples in later sections. Explanations relying on reason break down into arguments that rest on pure deductive reasoning alone and those based on the premise that a consideration of the world around us provides evidence of God's existence. This indirect evidence may be contrasted with the direct evidence of divine revelation that some theologians claim God makes available to true believers.

As for justifications for God's existence that eschew reason, some are concerned with rejecting the idea that we can "reason our way to God," so to speak. Rejecting the idea that belief in God's existence is, or can be, justified on the basis of reason or evidence is inevitably to accept such belief as a matter of faith. Perhaps the most famous proponent of this line of thought was the Danish philosopher Søren Kierkegaard (1813–55), who suggested that we have a vital need to believe in God, but denied that reason has any role to play in accounting for this need or explaining God's existence. We shall examine his views more closely in a later section of this chapter.

Another, more pragmatic approach, is the view that, at least for some people, certain psychological needs are fulfilled by believing in God. This approach downplays the question of the veracity of either belief in God or the matter of God's existence, and focuses instead on the functions and motivations such beliefs contribute to our overall set of beliefs or psychological profiles. There is no doubt that religion does indeed satisfy the needs of many people, and we shall return to a discussion of these needs on the final section of this chapter. Having sketched in outline some of the more widely recognized reasons for believing or not believing in God, let us explore these reasons in more detail in the next three sections.

6.2: Anselm's "Ontological Argument" for the Existence of God

In this and the following two sections we take a closer look at some of the most prominent and historically influential arguments that have been propounded for the existence of God. Provided they are sound, philosophical arguments ideally ought to convince whoever thinks about them in an impartial manner, but it is a curious feature of arguments for the existence of God, in my experience at least, that this rarely happens. More commonly, the arguments tend to be either flatly rejected as invalid or at best unsound by people who, for whatever reason, are predisposed to disbelieve in God's existence, accepted as self-evident by those who happen to have a prior belief in God based on the argument under consideration, or else dismissed as fatuous by the literal "defenders of the faith" who deny that rationality has anything to do with belief in God. Regardless, let us consider some of these time-honored arguments, beginning with a famous argument proposed by St. Anselm, the so-called *Ontological Argument*.

St. Anselm, who for a time held the prestigious position of Archbishop of Canterbury, proposed an argument that he thought provides conclusive proof of God's existence. A simplified version of Anselm's argument, consisting of two premises and a conclusion, reads as follows:

1. A being than which none greater exists can be conceived.
2. It is greater for such a being to exist actually than for it to exist merely in our imaginations.
3. Therefore such a being actually exists.

The being to which Anselm refers in this argument is God. Anselm's argument is an exercise in pure, deductive reasoning, meaning that the conclusion is meant to follow with absolute logical certainty from the premises. He intends to demonstrate that God's existence can be adduced on the basis of logic alone, but what exactly does the argument mean, and what are we to make of it? In order to answer these questions we must delve into the argument line by line.

In saying that "a being than which none greater exists can be conceived," Anselm is appealing to us to acknowledge that, if we only care to admit it, we possess the idea of some sort of supreme being. For good reason, he carefully avoids characterizing this supreme being in any positive terms. To do so is to invite someone to counter that he or she can conceive of some even greater being. In this sense, trying to characterize a supreme being is like trying to write down the highest number, which is also a futile exercise, since anyone can always add one to that number and thereby instantly trump the original number with a higher one. At any rate, let us grant for argument's sake that Anselm is right to claim that we can indeed relate to the idea of a supreme being in the sense he means.

The second premise of the argument asserts that implicit in the idea of any such being is the idea that it actually exists, for if such an entity were only a figment of our imagination, it would not be as great as one that exists in reality and not merely in our imagination. Now there is a sense in which Anselm has a point. I can conceive of having a million dollars, but a friend of mine who really is a millionaire is definitely richer than I, a millionaire only in my dreams. It is far greater, in this case, to have some property in reality than it is merely to conceive of having that property, a point my bank manager appreciates only too well.

Leaving the truth of the second premise to one side for a moment, it is fair to say that the conclusion follows from the two premises. That is, given the premises for the sake of argument, the conclusion follows from them. To this extent, Anselm's argument is valid. However, as we saw in Chapter Two, this in itself does not make an argument particularly interesting or worthy of serious attention. The question is this: is it a *sound* argument? For an argument to be sound, it must be both valid and have all true premises. Not surprisingly, given the objection we mentioned above, philosophers and logicians who deny the soundness of the

Ontological Argument usually reject the second premise as false. After all, why should we agree that *objects* are "greater" or "more perfect" if they exist in reality rather than hypothetically? In mathematics, geometers deal with perfect, ideal forms like circles and points, but the circles we actually draw are not at all more perfect than imaginary circles; in fact, the opposite is the case. So something that really exists is not necessarily always more perfect than an imaginary entity. In any case, it is far from obvious that existence is a property of something in the same way that, say, being red or being heavy is a property of something. Anselm may be right about the existence of God, but as it stands the truth of the second premise is dubious.

If we accept the form of Anselm's argument as it is presented, then it would seem to follow that any object we could conceive of as perfect would automatically have to exist in actuality. It would seem that a perfect island—strictly speaking, "an island than which none greater can be conceived"—a perfect tomato sandwich, a perfect Big Mac, and so on, would all exist in reality, given the form of Anselm's argument. One response to this would be to insist that these hypothetical objects are not really perfect because they are all limited in one way or another and that the only really perfect object is one that encompasses *all* perfections, namely God. But the problem with this rejoinder is that it seems to expose the entire argument to be *begging the question*; that is, the response seems to rely on smuggling the assumption of God's existence into the premises of the argument, rather than deriving this conclusion from the premises, as is the case in a properly formulated argument.

The Ontological Argument was resurrected by Descartes in a slightly different form, famously criticized by Kant, and has been the subject of ongoing controversy since Anselm first presented it. For some it represents a brilliant and elegant argument for God's existence, while for others it is a baffling and infuriating piece of logical bafflegab. For all that, however, it remains a benchmark in the history of debates about the existence of God.

6.3: St. Thomas Aquinas and the "Five Ways"

One of the most illustrious theologians and philosophers of all time, Aquinas was a thirteenth-century Dominican friar who was born in Italy but lived and taught extensively in Paris, where he held a university professorship in theology beginning in 1256. Aquinas wrote prodigiously on a range of metaphysical and Biblical subjects, but is remembered mainly as the author of two great theological tomes, the *Summa theologica* and the *Summa contra Gentiles*, which spell out in detail his religious philosophy. These works have had an enormous impact on the course of Christian thought, particularly Catholic theology. The significance of Aquinas's contribution to the philosophy of religion consists primarily in his ingenious efforts to reconcile Aristotle's philosophy with Christianity and in his famous *Five Ways*, which are five succinct arguments purporting to prove the existence of God.

Aquinas's Five Ways can be roughly divided into two groups: the first four, which comprise variations on what has become known as the Cosmological Argument, and the last one, which is called the Teleological Argument. Aquinas distinguished between faith in God and reason, and although he did not think that any contradiction arises between what God may reveal of himself to true believers and what we discover of God's existence through the exercise of our reason, his aim in the Five Ways is to persuade us that God's existence can be demonstrated on the basis of a combination of reason and reflection on the natural world. I think it is helpful to think of Aquinas's Five Ways as falling into a category of arguments called *inferences to the best explanation*. Such arguments consist of premises that identify observations standing in need of some sort of explanation, and conclusions that are supposed to provide the best available explanations of those observations.

In the first Way, Aquinas begins by inviting us to consider the fact that certain things in the world are in motion. Things that are in motion are caused to move by other things, which in turn are in motion due to the motion of other objects, and so on. But what is at the beginning of this chain of motion? Aquinas cannot accept that the chain of objects in motion stretches back indefinitely in time with no beginning. Were there no fixed beginning, then there would be nothing to make the motions of bodies anything other than *relative* motions. There must, he thinks, be some sort of first, or prime, mover, and this first mover, he states, is what we understand to be God. The actual argument is a little more involved than the version I present here, but this is the gist of it.

The second Way basically generalizes the first and focuses on the nature of cause—strictly speaking "efficient cause," a term he took from Aristotle—and effect. An event or thing in the world is brought about by its cause, which in turn is brought about by some prior cause, and so on. Since nothing we have experienced is self-caused, there must be some end to this series of causes and effects stretching back into the past. Again, there must be some first cause, and this first cause, according to Aquinas, is what we call God. Unlike objects or events in nature, Aquinas takes God to be self-caused and the original source of all causes and motions in the world.

The first two Ways expose Aquinas's heavy debt to the now antiquated physics and metaphysics of Aristotle, especially in the aversion Aquinas exhibits to the idea of infinite processes that lack starting points, and in his postulation of a prime mover. The third Way trades on the concepts of possibility and necessity. Aquinas says that some things are possible, in the sense that they exist at one time but not at all times. But it is not possible that *all* things are merely possible in this sense, since then, he claims, there would have been a time when none of these possible things existed. But nothing comes from nothing, and since there are clearly things that exist now, there must also be some necessary being, some entity the existence of which is necessary. We call this necessary being God. The weak link in this argument is the inference that if the world were to consist of nothing but possible beings, then there would have to be a time at which the non-existence of all these beings coincides. This part of the argument appears to be dubious at best.

The fourth Way also turns on some outdated physics and is perhaps the least interesting of them all, but the fifth Way, also called the *argument from design*, is one of the most enduring arguments for God's existence. Again closely following Aristotle, Aquinas notes that objects in the world "act for an end" or purpose, even though things in nature themselves typically lack intelligence. In fact, this only goes to show that some intelligence is required to direct inanimate objects, since "the arrow is directed by the archer," to use his words. There must, then, be some intelligent being lurking behind the natural order and directing things to their ends, a being which is God.

This "argument from design" is certainly one of the more powerful, subtle, and compelling of arguments devised by theists, and it has enjoyed several reincarnations in the history of philosophy. For example, the theologian William Paley (1743–1805) invited us to ponder what our reaction should be if we were to come across a watch lying on the ground. Is it plausible to suppose that the intricate mechanism of a watch somehow came into existence by chance, or should we rather interpret this intricacy as evidence of a watchmaker who designed the watch? Like Aristotle and Aquinas before him, Paley saw evidence of order and purpose in the world, and like many other theists, attributed this order to a creative intelligence or designer we call God.

Design arguments, however, are also vulnerable to a number of powerful objections. One problem with these types of arguments is that, like beauty, evidence of design in the natural world seems to be very much in the eye of the beholder. If the world around us manifests order, then surely it also displays signs of disorder, and so one might well ask: In comparison with *what* is the world orderly? Moreover, could not an intelligent designer have made some obvious improvements to the earth we inhabit, for example by having created one free of earthquakes and other natural disasters? David Hume levelled scathing criticisms against the argument along these lines in his posthumously published *Dialogues on Natural Religion*. Evidence of design also needs to be interpreted with care when it comes to ascertaining what constitutes design and what is merely an adaptation to pre-existing circumstances. For example, a watch is clearly evidence of the work of an intelligent watchmaker, but watches are fitted with straps so that we can wear them on our arms. The intelligence of the design of watchstraps makes sense when viewed in this light. To argue that the designer of arms must have been intelligent to design arms perfectly suited to wearing watches is faulty reasoning because it puts the cart before the horse, so to speak. Critics maintain that proponents of arguments from design make exactly the same mistake of putting the cart before the horse in construing the natural order as evidence of an intelligent designer. The criticism is that we impose order and design arbitrarily and in our own image.

But if we grant the force of these criticisms, how else might we account for the incredible complexity of, say, a chimpanzee, which is far more intricate and impressive an entity than any human invention? Before the advent of Darwin's theory of evolution, this was indeed a deep mystery, but modern biology has given us an alternative way of understanding how highly complex organisms can evolve. This understanding is based on the biological processes of reproduction, mutation, and natural selection, as well as sufficient time. The real significance of the theory of evolution is its ability to explain how chance mechanisms acting against the backdrop of the natural environment can generate the organisms we find in the biosphere. As a result, the design argument has lost some of its force in the last century, although some theists respond that the origins and progress of evolution themselves stand in need of some sort of purposive explanation and that Darwin's theory is quite compatible with a purposeful universe created by an intelligent God.

6.4: KIERKEGAARD'S LEAP OF FAITH AND PASCAL'S WAGER

Søren Kierkegaard's philosophy of religion grew out of his perception that Christian life in nineteenth-century Denmark was complacent and sterile. Fervently opposed to all attempts to prove the existence of God by reason as exercises in futility, Kierkegaard flatly rejected the idea of pursuing objective truths about God, espousing instead that committing oneself to God is a subjective and passionate leap of faith. God is unknowable, according to Kierkegaard, and the point of religion is not to arrive at truths or to know, but rather to believe. Indeed, he freely admitted that the doctrines of Christianity and faith are irrational and absurd. What, then, motivates anyone to submit to faith in God in the first place? For Kierkegaard, this is a matter of confronting our fear of death and our deep, inner feelings of smallness and insignificance in the face of the vastness of eternity. To face these feelings honestly is to acknowledge our need for God and the vital interest we have in God's existence.

But while Kierkegaard's confessions are refreshingly candid and his willingness to concede that faith in God is irrational is courageous, there is little in his philosophy to commend itself to anyone who does not already believe in God. His message may resonate with Christians able to identify with his view of a subjective, passionate relationship with God, as well as with the suffering and needs he professed. However, if faith in God is as subjective and personal a matter as Kierkegaard claims, then surely this faith is little more than a strictly take-it-or-leave-it affair, rather than something that necessarily has meaning or significance for everyone.

Another route to God, although one less concerned with assuming God's existence or trying to prove it than with urging that belief in God is prudent, is advanced by the French philosopher and mathematician Blaise Pascal (1623–62). Pascal's argument, which closely resembles what is known as a *payoff matrix* in the mathematical study of game theory, is elegant and thought provoking. The argument is known as *Pascal's Wager* and it goes as follows. There are two possible scenarios regarding the reality of God: either God exists or God does not exist. And let us also suppose we have two choices open to us: we can either believe in God or not. These possibilities, each pair of which is said to describe "mutually exclusive and exhaustive" scenarios, generate four combinations: God exists and we correctly believe in God; God exists and we don't believe; God doesn't exist and we falsely believe in God; and God doesn't exist and we don't believe. Pascal also assumes orthodox Christian doctrines about heaven and hell, God's desire that we be believers and the consequences of our choices concerning belief in God's existence. The "payoffs" for us of these four possibilities are as follows. In the first case—that is, God exists and we believe—we receive the ultimate prize of eternal life. In the second case, we are faced with a worst-case scenario, assuming that God is vengeful and punishes with eternal damnation whomever doesn't believe. The third case, where we commit ourselves to belief in a non-existent God, would mean we harmlessly devote our lives to performing Christian duties and virtues, while the last scenario, in which God doesn't exist and we're not believers anyway, is simply the "nothing ventured, nothing gained" of the *status quo*.

Weighing up the outcomes of these cases in terms of whether we should decide to become believers, Pascal's Wager is that we should be believers. He reasoned that the potential downside of not believing, which is damnation and an eternity in hell, is far outweighed by the payoff for believing, which offers at the very worst a life spent making mild sacrifices in the worship of a non-existent God, and at best offers heavenly bliss after death. Given his assumptions, Pascal makes an excellent case for this gambler's strategy, but is this strategy a pious or praiseworthy reason for believing in God? Certainly it is no part of conventional Christianity that we should believe in God on purely selfish grounds, although Pascal's Wager would seem to be a sensible and prudent bet, given the Christian doctrines he assumes. Sincere theists, however, tend to find Pascal's argument cynical and disturbing. In casting the issue of belief as a matter of optimizing one's gambling strategy, Pascal seems to reduce belief in God to a crude form of manipulation. In any case, if we accept Pascal's Wager and the logic he employs, would we not be compelled to give up belief in God and wager instead on some other hypothetical deity that exerts an even greater appeal than God? For example, imagine a deity exactly like Pascal's God in every respect, except that this other deity requires nothing from us in terms of worship and sacrifice. Call this entity Godplus. Godplus is easy to conceive and fits conveniently into Pascal's payoff matrix, and there would arguably be even stronger grounds for believing in Godplus than there are to believe in God. When viewed in this light, Pascal's Wager ironically becomes as good a rationale *not* to believe in God as it is to become a believer.

The American philosopher and psychologist William James (1842–1910) gave a somewhat similar explanation of the benefits that belief in God has to offer. Given that we do not know whether God really exists, and that we are unlikely to settle the issue one way or another, given also how much belief in God promises to the faithful, and given that not believing in God offers us so little compensation in comparison, it only makes sense to give theists the benefit of the doubt and believe in God. "If religion be true," James writes in *The Will to Believe*, "and the evidence for it be still insufficient, I do not wish ... to forfeit my sole chance in life of getting on the winning side." But James's pragmatic attitude towards belief in God, while unassailable if we think of the issue purely as a kind of business decision, is no more intellectually satisfying than Pascal's Wager. Not only is James's cavalier disregard of the truth in what is for many people a profound ontological question disquieting, but, like Pascal's Wager, the appeal of James's reasons for believing in God seems to consist mainly in the refuge it offers to cowards and the insecure.

6.5: GOD'S CRITICS

Having considered some of the standard arguments and reasons for believing in God, let us now turn to some salient reasons philosophers have given for not believing. Non-believers in God can be roughly divided into those who believe that God does not exist—and those who think we do not have sufficient reason to believe in such a God, or at least insufficient reason given our present knowledge. The former are known as *atheists* and the latter *agnostics*. Most of the philosophers we discuss in this section are atheists who propose various explanations why belief in God has historically exerted a strong spell over many people. Needless to say, there has been no shortage of critics of God and religion in general throughout history, especially since the time of the eighteenth-century Enlightenment, when openly opposing the Church started to become safer. In this section we will touch on the views of Marx, Nietzsche, and Freud, and consider one other approach to explaining the extraordinary resilience that belief in God has enjoyed through the ages.

Karl Marx (1818–83) is remembered primarily as the political, economic, and social theorist who, together with Friedrich Engels (1820–95), changed the course of world history with his enormously influential advocacy of socialism and communism. Marx saw economic and historical forces as responsible for shaping human ideologies and institutions, including religion, which he took to be invented by humans, not a reflection of any higher power or spiritual realm. Viewed in these materialistic, secular terms, Marx thought that although religion offers us moral foundations and a general theory of the world, it functions as an insidious escape for the masses from their lot in life, which is a state of economic oppression. Religion, to use the famous phrase he coined, is the opium of the people, a comforting illusion which keeps us from seizing control of our destinies and creating our own happiness by changing the material conditions of our lives.

Like Marx, the polemical German philosopher Friedrich

Nietzsche insisted that the ability of humankind to achieve greatness lies in our hands and ours alone. However, unlike Marx, Nietzsche was driven less by political ideology than by outright contempt for Christianity, which he singled out as a particularly reprehensible religion. In his unmistakably vehement and scornful prose style, Nietzsche denounced Christianity as a religion for the sick, weak, and impotent, dismissing the Christian God as a loathsome object of worship. Far from ennobling us or holding out promise for our eventual salvation, Christianity, according to Nietzsche, succeeds only in destroying what is worthy about the human spirit. "God is dead," he declared, and he rejoiced at the prospect that Christianity was showing signs of waning during his own time. But while Christianity is strictly a religion for losers as far as Nietzsche is concerned, his real targets are ideologies like democracy and humanitarianism that involve the subordination or subservience of the human will. He likened humankind outgrowing religion to the way a child outgrows its childhood clothes. Notwithstanding these withering attacks, it is Nietzsche who is dead now, and if anything God's worldwide popularity ratings remain as high as they were when Nietzsche finally shed his mortal coil.

The fertile ground of psychoanalysis offers another avenue for understanding and explaining the attraction of belief in God, while at the same time casting doubt on the reality of God's existence. The founder of psychoanalysis, Sigmund Freud (1856–1939), sought to locate the origins of religious belief in our inner psychological urges and wishes. In particular, Freud suggested that childhood needs for protection and love, as well as our deep-seated feelings of helplessness, are responsible for what he calls the illusion of belief in God. Of course, the needs he talks about are to some extent met by parental figures, especially fathers, but Freud theorized that God functions as a kind of super father-figure, one which also gratifies our longings for justice, a secure moral order and immortality. So on this account, belief in God is a matter of *wish fulfillment* in relation to these needs, needs which real father figures can only satisfy partially.

Another explanation for the longevity and tenacity of belief in God, not altogether dissimilar to Freud's theory but with a more anthropological orientation, has recently emerged from the social sciences. The idea is that the concept of divine or supernatural authority originated in the distant past of societies based on hunting and gathering as a ploy utilized by the leaders of bands and tribes to bolster and legitimize their own authority. The theory holds that a potentially insecure alpha-male would have found it extremely useful to claim some kind of special connection to a higher, supreme power, especially one endowed with extraordinary powers of wrath and vengeance in case the wishes of its earthly representative were disobeyed. Indeed, the enormously powerful political instrument known as the *divine right of kings* survived in European monarchies until relatively recent times. Over time this ploy, which could well have arisen independently and in various forms in different societies, evolved into deities that became objects of worship in their own right. From an anthropological perspective, this theory neatly explains not only the prevalence of, but also the fear so commonly associated with, beliefs in supernatural beings in cultures around the world. In addition, this account gives us a plausible, alternative explanation of why the characterizations of so many gods are closely linked to masculine imagery and virtues, a recurring theme in many religions and one that Freud, as we have seen, also tries to explain.

This last account of how and why beliefs in supernatural beings originated and propagated in human societies makes for an interesting comparison with an idea put forward some years ago by the English zoologist Richard Dawkins (1941–) in his book *The Selfish Gene*. After making a case for the idea that Darwinian evolution operates at the level of the propagation of genes rather than individual organisms, Dawkins makes the bold claim that a process analogous to Darwinism takes place in the human intellectual sphere. His idea is that ideas compete for survival in the context of human culture, just as genes compete for survival in the gene pool. He calls these units of ideas *memes*. Viewed in these terms, we might consider the idea of God to be a particularly successful meme, one that has managed to take root in very many human societies and has proved extremely durable and adaptable, not unlike a highly resilient gene. Whether Dawkins is stretching the metaphors of competition, selection, and survival too far is a moot point, but to consider the influence and role of God as an idea is, if nothing else, highly thought-provoking.

6.6: THE PROBLEM OF EVIL

Misfortunes of all kinds befall us in life, from minor adversities to natural disasters to evil deeds and crimes perpetrated by our fellow humans. Disasters like these and others present us with various hardships, but when we speak of the problem of evil in the context of philosophy and theology, we do not refer to any one particular calamity or evil. Rather, the problem of evil refers to the paradox that apparently arises due to the existence of evil in the world and the properties that God is supposed to possess as a supreme being. In this section, we examine this difficulty and consider some possible solutions to it.

Among the properties theologians typically claim God manifests are the following three:

> God is omnipotent (or all-powerful).
> God is omniscient (or all-knowing).
> God is all-loving.

The problem arises when we attempt to reconcile a God embodying all of these properties with the existence of evil in the world. If God is all-powerful, for example, then it surely follows that God has the power to prevent evil and suffering from occurring in the world; and if God is all-knowing, that means God presumably knows everything that happens to us in the past, present, and future. It seems to follow from this that since clearly evil and suffering do take place, God must be fully aware of whatever evils and sufferings are in store for us in life. But how could a God who is also supposed to be all-loving tolerate such a state of affairs?

Suppose you take your pet dog for a walk and the dog strays close to some passing traffic. If you can see that your dog is in harm's way, and you have the power to do something to prevent the harm—by pulling on the leash, for example—*and* you love your dog, you would surely be cruel and heartless to allow your dog to be hit by a vehicle. Your relationship with the dog is analogous to God's relationship with us, except of course that God is supposed to have even greater powers to prevent suffering than we do. The property of omniscience appears to lead to other complications as well, for it is far from obvious that we have genuine free will if God knows all along exactly what we are going to do, but we will leave this issue to one side.

The attempt to reconcile the problem of evil with God is known as *theodicy*. The problem is easily averted if we sacrifice any of the three properties attributed to God above. The trouble with moves along these lines, though, is that they inevitably leave us with a God that is less impressive and less admirable than we might expect, and one that is conspicuously inferior to Anselm's being "than which none greater can be conceived." Short of compromising God's divine attributes, perhaps the most celebrated theodicy is an argument due to Leibniz. Leibniz argues that having created a world with some evil in it is not only compatible with God's plan, but is in fact a necessary component of the optimal world God intended to create, a world of maximal variety and liberty. Our world is, to use his famous expression, "the best of all possible worlds," notwithstanding the presence of evil all around us. According to this view, evil is not a sign of any failure or weakness on God's part, but a part of His divine plan. This argument is closely related to the credible point that without any evil in the world we would have no sense of the nature of good and therefore no motivation to strive to be good ourselves.

But Leibniz's apology for the existence of evil invites some fairly obvious questions. Why do we need to be exposed to so much evil in order to appreciate good? Why do we have to endure pain and suffering that do not result from any moral shortcomings on our part and that seem to hold no moral lessons for us, such as the misery visited upon us by earthquakes, new forms of disease, and so on? If God's intention is that we learn certain lessons about making the right moral choices, why do the teaching methods have to be so harsh and arbitrary? And if these lessons have to do with paying for sins originally committed by our ancestors, how just is it to continue to punish every new generation for these transgressions? Exactly what do famines or droughts tell us about the existence of a beneficent God?

The problem of evil inevitably comes down to a matter of reconciling the power of an ostensibly omnipotent God with the existence of evil. One way of resolving this difficulty is to admit that the power of God is compromised by evil. The Manichaeans, who were a Babylonian religious cult founded by Mani (216–77), advanced one such strategy. Manichaeans believed that God, represented physically in the world by light, is locked in a titanic struggle with Satan, represented by darkness. There are interesting parallels between this dualistic conception of good and evil as competing forces and ideas in certain Eastern religions. The Manichaean doctrine also has the virtue of affirming our sense that good and evil complement each other. However, the teachings of the Manichaeans exert little influence today, possibly because orthodox theists regard the fundamental duality of good and evil as posing too great a threat to God's omnipotence.

Other than claiming that we must simply put our faith in a God who works in inscrutable ways, theists have few solutions to the problem of evil. But while philosophers are certainly used to questions that do not have satisfactory answers, they are entitled to feel frustrated by riddles that can only have unsatisfactory answers, which is precisely what theodicies appear to be.

6.7: Religion, Death, and the Meanings of Life

When people give their reasons for attending church, practicing religion, or worshipping God, a recurring theme is that these beliefs and practices bestow meaning or purpose on their lives. And indeed, religious language speaks to our profound desire to know that our lives have meaning. After all, this language is laden with references to concepts such as a higher purpose, a spiritual calling, God's plan for us, and the rewards and punishments that await us in the afterlife and reflect the way we conduct ourselves in this life. But what does the meaning of life reside in, and to what extent can religious beliefs confer meaning to our lives?

For many of us, a sense of futility and despair comes with reflection upon the meaning or purpose of our lives, and originates in our confrontation with the prospect of our eventual death. We fear death, but barring so-called near death experiences, we never actually experience death while we are alive, and none of us knows for certain that we will experience anything after we die. However, it is perfectly understandable that we fear the pain and debility that often accompany death, and also that we fear death as representing the unknown. In addition, the fact that our life is transient suggests that it is of no importance in the grand scheme of things.

Life is a zero-sum game, in that we come into it with nothing, and we take nothing with us when we leave. Given this, what is the point in striving to be good, changing the world for the better, amassing great fortunes, struggling to do as much as we can or trying to be the best we can, if all our efforts are destined to dissipate in the trackless desert of time when our time is up? We leave monuments in our name, write poems or songs, make bequests, and bear children in our attempt to extend our intellectual and biological legacy beyond our graves, but even these efforts seem doomed in the long run, especially if, as many astrophysicists now think, the universe is headed for a long, slow death in a losing battle with gravity and entropy.

Prolonging life by carefully attending to our health or spending money on expensive therapies can postpone one's demise for a while, but the extra time we purchase amounts to no more than a momentary blip in the vast reaches of eternity. The infant technology of cryogenics, or freezing living organisms and bringing them back to life, does big business in California by trading on our readiness to bet that medical science will one day find a way to vanquish death. And at least some religions, as Pascal pointedly reminds us, offer the ultimate payoff of blissful and eternal life after death. So everyone, it seems, wants to beat death, but to what end? This might seem like a silly question; nonetheless, who hasn't felt wistful about how another lifetime would allow us to do all the things we cannot possibly squeeze into a measly 80 years, whether it be studying Spanish, mastering the piano, or travelling to remote corners of the planet? But how many lifetimes would be enough? Three? 68? 1,057? Might we not simply reach a point when we would want to cry out: "Enough is enough?" The familiar adage "so much to do; so little time" would conceivably turn into the no less distressing lament: "so little to do; too much time" if our craving for immortality is ever satisfied. We should, as the proverb goes, be careful about what we wish for.

The point is that, unless our lives already have meaning, it is not clear that more life will magically supply it, nor is it clear that cramming more activity into our lives will invest them with more meaning. This is where religions appear to fill a niche, because they often articulate the meaning of our lives in terms of the roles we play in some divine plan or purpose. But this only invites the question: What is the purpose of divinities such as God? Similar questions also arise, by the way, for the various Cosmological Arguments of Aquinas. God is supposed to be the First Cause and the Prime Mover, but we are quite entitled to ask: What causes or moves God? Apart from bluntly insisting that God is the one and only self-caused, self-sufficient and immutable entity in existence, theists have no satisfactory answers to offer non-theists. For non-theists, then, what prospect is there that life has any meaning at all?

The basic difference in outlook concerning the meaning of life between believers in God on the one hand, and atheists and agnostics on the other, appears to come down to this: for believers the meaning of life tends to be a matter of revelation, whereas for atheists and agnostics whatever meaning life might hold tends to be a human creation. That is, believers maintain that the source of the meaning of life is external to themselves and is to be discovered in religion in general and God in particular, while for non-believers, meaning in life is at best a product of whatever personal, humanitarian or other secular agenda they manage to carry out. A life spent working to alleviate the plight of starving refugees may be more meaningful for some than a life spent watching television, but it is more meaningful only relative to human concerns and interests. None of our most noble endeavors would appear to be any match for the crushing oblivion of time. This prospect is a source of despair for some, to be sure, but only if we allow ourselves to succumb to despair. It is, like much in life, a matter of attitude. Happily for believers, second thoughts and misgivings of this sort enter the picture far less. Theists, disciples, and religious followers have at least the security that an external, objective meaning attaches to their lives. Whether this security is warranted is another matter entirely, and some believers have been known to undergo psychological stress if they experience a crisis of faith, but fixed reference points of this sort are certainly not the least of religion's attractions.

Earlier in this section we posed the question: What is the meaning of life? Rather than supposing there to be a single, simple answer to this question, what I am suggesting is that there are instead multiple meanings of life. Some of us look within ourselves to find or create them, while others discover them in outside sources such as scriptures or the teachings of gurus. Some meanings of life, that is to say, are subjective, while others are objective; some are open-ended and changeable, while others are eternal and fixed goals we set our sights upon. Our dispositions, temperaments, attitudes, and outlooks upon life go a long way to explaining the routes we take in the search for meaning, but regardless of where and how we pursue, find, discover or create meanings in our lives, what it is we undergo in the process and where this process leads do perhaps more than anything in defining our lives to ourselves and to those around us.

6.8: CONCLUSION

This brings to a close our glance at the philosophy of religion. That we have shed very little new light on the status of religious pronouncements or the existence of God should come as no surprise. The key claims of religion, such as those having to do with an afterlife or the existence of God, are notoriously difficult to test scientifically, and therefore they tend to remain immune to refutation. Contrast this with the view of the late philosopher of science Sir Karl Popper (1902–94), who took it to be a defining characteristic of science that its hypotheses are at least potentially falsifiable. This does not mean that religious claims are untrue, nor does it mean we have no reason whatsoever to think that God exists. As the saying goes, absence of evidence is not evidence of absence. Indeed, it is even possible that God does exist but deliberately chooses to keep us guessing about His existence. If so, then it is impossible for us to prove or disprove God's existence, and it should be left up to each of us to decide whether it is more plausible to believe in such a resolutely reclusive God than to concur with Xenophanes, Hume, Freud, and other doubters that it is more likely than not that we create deities in our own image.

Not surprisingly, we have neither proved nor disproved God's existence, and the issue is never likely to be settled decisively. Anselm, Aquinas, Pascal, Kierkegaard, and James all articulate reasons for believing in God's existence, while Marx, Freud, Dawkins, and others seek rather to understand and explain why belief in God endures so tenaciously, even though they themselves find no compelling evidence for God's existence. As a general principle, however, we are wise not to accept blindly just any claim put before us, irrespective of how much it promises, unless we have the strongest of reasons to accept it. And so, just as we exercise our critical faculties when it comes to the existence of the tooth fairy or the extravagant claims of real estate agents in Florida, we are well advised to be no less critical when it comes to the glad tidings of theists. While we may be unable to prove theists wrong, we do ourselves no favour by burdening ourselves with worthless swamps, even if those swamps come with heavenly bonus offers.

CHAPTER 7

Some Metaphysical Musings

[The world] is neither a universe pure and simple nor a manyverse pure and simple.

— WILLIAM JAMES

7.0: OBJECTIVITY, SUBJECTIVITY, REALISM, ANTIREALISM, AND TRUTH

In this chapter, which you should treat as optional for the purposes of introductory reading material, I enlarge upon some of the major themes of the preceding chapters, beginning with the Introduction and the discussion of starting points in philosophy. You may recall that I argued there that, when we set out to pursue answers to philosophical questions, we are faced at the very outset with making a choice between *objective* and *subjective* starting points, and that this decision can bear crucially on the answers we are likely to find. In this section, I relate this idea to the distinction between *metaphysical realism* and *antirealism*.

As I briefly mentioned in Chapter One, realism in metaphysics is simply the view that reality is external to us and exists independently of our minds. According to realists, we find ourselves inhabiting such a world, a world that does not depend for its existence on humans. Another way of putting this is to say that realists take the existence of the world to be objective rather than subjective. The specific nature of what realists claim exists independently of us vary according to the stripe of realist in question. For example, a scientific realist looks to science to provide an account of the furniture of the world; for an orthodox theist, God's existence at the very least is objective and real; a realist about mathematics claims that mathematical objects, such as sets or numbers, really exist; an ethical realist thinks that at least one moral good or evil is absolute and at least in some sense independent of us, regardless of differences among societies, cultures or individuals, and so on. In its weakest, most basic form, metaphysical realism does not entail the objective existence of any one *specific* entity or entities; rather it is simply a commitment to the idea that there is *some* sort of objective reality, whatever shape or form reality might take. For reasons we articulated in our discussion of Kant in Chapter Three, there are powerful reasons for denying that what we can describe a world outside of our minds with any confidence. Metaphysical realism, however, can accommodate a high degree of skepticism about the exact nature of whatever one takes to exist independently of us. Realism is compatible with a world comprising physical objects, elementary particles, events, Platonic Forms, spiritual entities, all of the above, some combination of the above, or even none of the above. The objective perspective upon which realism is predicated has been variously referred to as the God's-eye point of view (by Hilary Putnam), the view from nowhere (by Thomas Nagel), and the Archimedean point, after the ancient mathematician Archimedes (*c.* 290–*c.* 212 B.C.E.), who reputedly lamented that if he had had but one firm spot on which to stand, he could have moved the earth.

In direct contrast, antirealists deny that the world is mind-independent, arguing instead that reality is a construction of, or in some other way dependent on, the human mind. Antirealism bears a superficial resemblance to idealism, but the two should not be confused. Idealists like Bishop Berkeley take the nature of reality to be mind-like, as opposed to material, but from this it does not follow that reality is *human* mind-dependent. In fact, Berkeley was adamant that God's existence is real and objective, and in this sense he too was a metaphysical realist. On the other hand, if nothing exists outside of human minds, then reality itself is necessarily mind-like. Protagoras succinctly stated the basic tenet of antirealism in his famous dictum: *Humans are the measure of all things.* In rejecting metaphysical realism, the antirealist is thereby committed to rejecting the idea of objectivity and the existence of anything objective. Antirealists are committed subjectivists. They think that subjectivity is inescapable, that it exhausts reality, and that the subjective perspective alone is available to us.

Toward the end of Chapter Two, I intimated that there is a close connection between metaphysical realism and what I called the objective, or ontological conception of truth. We are now in a position to make this connection explicit. I claim that the idea of an objective perspective is tantamount to subscribing to an objective conception of truth, and so commitment to metaphysical realism is at the same time a commitment to an ontological conception of truth. The link between the two is this. By taking at least one thing to exist objectively and independently of us, the metaphysical realist is in effect claiming that there is *a way that things are*, or *an objective fact of the matter*. But that there is an objective fact of the matter about some aspect of the world is precisely what a proponent of the ontological conception of truth means by truth. For her, truth just *is* this objective state of affairs, no more and no less, and so the two theories—one about the nature of existence and the other about the nature of truth—actually coincide. Conversely, to accept that truth indeed lies outside the human mind, which is what the ontological theorist of truth asserts, amounts to affirming that humans are *not* the measure of all things, which is just what the metaphysical realist maintains. We must remember that it does not follow from this that anyone actually *knows* any specific, objective truths. Rather, the point is that metaphysical realism and the conception of truth as being objective in nature entail each other, and that a commitment to either of them ultimately comes down to an article of faith. I should add that while the correspondence theory of truth also presupposes metaphysical realism, one can reject the correspondence theory without rejecting realism, whereas to reject the ontological conception of truth *is* to reject metaphysical realism.

Antirealism, then, which involves denying the idea that truth is objective, goes hand in hand with a purely subjective conception of truth. The archetypal subjective theory of truth is relativism: the view that one person's or society's truth is no more credible than any other's, even if two claims directly contradict each other. We know from our survey of theories of truth in Chapter Two, however, that theories of truth are not restricted to relativism and the ontological theory alone. The pragmatic and coherence theories are examples of alternative theories. How do such theories fare in terms of my characterization of theories of truth as either objective or subjective? To the extent that such theories reject the objectivity of truth, I suggest, their proponents face a serious credibility problem unless they can show how it is that those theories do not ultimately collapse into subjectivity.

The metaphysics of pure subjectivity means that, strictly speaking, nothing exists other than the human mind. But this amounts to nothing more than a kind of collective solipsism, or else just solipsism pure and simple. Indeed, I would suggest that antirealists—or pure subjectivists when it comes to truth for that matter—are faced with explaining how it is that they keep from sliding into solipsism. After all, to commit oneself entirely to subjectivity is just what it is to be a solipsist, and vice-versa! Note also that an objective conception of truth is unavailable to the solipsist: she cannot even claim that solipsism is really true, because by definition this "truth" cannot be grounded in any real, objective state of affairs. The most the solipsist can say is that solipsism is true *for her*. This is not a refutation of solipsism *per se*, because I have proved neither metaphysical realism nor the objectivity of truth; what I am refuting, rather, is the claim that solipsism is, or even can be, *objectively true*. While proponents of the pragmatic or coherence theory of truth are likely to renounce solipsism, I would suggest that the onus is on adherents of non-objective theories of truth to explain how their positions do not ultimately reduce to solipsism if they reject the objectivity of truth out of hand.

The implications of one's choice of objective versus subjective points of departure in philosophy should now be apparent. To begin philosophizing with an objective outlook will naturally incline one towards metaphysical realism and an objective conception of truth, while to adopt a subjective starting point tends to lead to antirealism and subjectivity with respect to truth. I have not argued that one starting point or metaphysical commitment is preferable, or superior, to the other. Rather, I am merely aiming to illuminate some consequences of the implicit choices involved at the outset when one undertakes philosophy.

7.1: THE ONE-MANY PROBLEM AND TRUTH

The oldest, and perhaps also the deepest and most universal of all philosophical questions, are metaphysical ones. Why does anything exist at all rather than nothing? No one has the answer, but an interesting way of turning that question on its head can be found in the whimsical definition of physics as the task of explaining why not everything happens at once! For whatever reason, there evidently *is* something rather than nothing, and so next we want to understand the nature of this something. Is the something that exists One—a single, unified, and indivisible entity—or is it a fragmented plurality of entities—a Many? In other words, does the universe consist of one thing or many things? This is the One-Many problem. Furthermore, if the universe consists of many things, are they all the same kind of thing or are there different sorts of things? And are the apparent differences between things real or illusory? In this section I explore some answers to these questions and relate those answers to the nature of truth and metaphysical realism.

It is a basic tenet of various mystical teachings, religions, and philosophies that *All is One*. That is, mystics the world over tend to maintain that reality is whole and unified; and the point of many mystical teachings is to provide seekers with a sense of oneness with the Cosmos, for example via practicing meditation or reflection for long periods of time. Ontologically speaking, the view that only one thing or substance exists and that everything is part of that one thing is known as *monism*. As we saw in Chapter One, Parmenides adopted exactly this position, as did Spinoza, although in Spinoza's more nuanced account, this one substance supposedly manifests itself in numerous modes of existence. Some versions of monism, such as Spinoza's, hold that the world is infinite, but this is not a necessary condition of monism. Similarly, monists tend to share an affinity with idealists, although again, idealism is not a necessary consequence of monism. Idealists take reality to be essentially mind-like, but this leaves open the possibility that reality consists of a collection of distinct, individual minds, which is not a variety of monism. On the other hand, an idealist who takes reality to consist of a single, indivisible mind is a monist.

To appreciate what monism is and what it means, consider a coin. From an external, objective perspective, the coin has two sides, and the difference between the sides is real. But from the perspective of the coin itself (or from some part of it), there is no such external perspective, and so differences in the world of the coin are all relative to, or internal to, the coin itself. Such differences, then, are apparent rather than real. If you were part of the coin (a conscious part, if you like), your reality would be limited strictly to coin-stuff, and as such, differences between the interior of the coin and its surface, or between parts of the coin and the coin as a whole, would be moot. For the monist, then, reality cannot be objective, and differences are ultimately relative to the one thing that the monist, by definition, is a part of.

The alternative to monism is ontological pluralism, the view that more than one thing exists. Pluralism comes in two main forms: one type of pluralism holds that different things exist, but that they are all things of the *same kind*, while the other asserts that in fact *different kinds* of things exist. The idealist who believes in the existence of a collection of distinct minds exemplifies the former, while a physicist who thinks that, for example, different kinds of elementary particles exist, falls into the latter category. Now one feature common to both types of pluralism is what I call the *independence principle*, which asserts that there must be at least one thing or entity that exists independently of at least one other thing or entity. To see why pluralism entails the independence principle, consider what it would mean to deny the independence principle. Denying this principle would mean that nothing can exist independently of anything else—in other words, it would mean that everything in existence is an essentially indivisible, self-supporting system, such that to subtract anything from it would mean that the whole system could no longer exist. But this is just another way of saying that, ontologically speaking, everything is an integral part of what it is that exists, which in turn is another way of saying that no one thing can exist without the existence of everything. This, however, is just to say that All is One, which is monism.

Let me say a little more about what the independence principle entails. It is simply the very weak claim that the existence of not all things is mutually interdependent. In other words, at least one thing must exist independently of some other thing. If the outside world exists independently of my mind, it does not follow that my mind exists independently of the world. But it does mean that the world and my mind are not the same thing, and that the difference between the two is real. For in this case we have something that exists autonomously (that is, the world) and something that exists dependently (that is, my mind). In other words, independence is not necessarily a reciprocal relation. Descartes is an example of one such ontological pluralist.

He holds that there are several kinds of substance, and that our existence is dependent on God, but that we nevertheless exist. The key point is that something—in this case God—exists independently of us, and of him in particular.

You might recall from Chapter One that talk of independence also entered into our original formulation of metaphysical realism. This is no coincidence. Remember, the metaphysical realist holds that at least some part of the world exists independently of human beings, a view that automatically satisfies the independence principle. In fact I claim that, just as ontological pluralism is predicated upon the independence principle, so too is metaphysical realism, because if not everything is human-mind dependent, which is what the metaphysical realist maintains, then it follows that at least one thing exists independently of humans, which is precisely what the independence principle requires. Conversely, if nothing is independent of anything else, then nothing can be independent of any human mind, *your* mind included. But this is just a statement of anti-realism. Antirealism, then, involves rejection of the independence principle.

But since metaphysical realism stands or falls with the ontological conception of truth I sketched in Chapter Two, and since realism is tied to the independence principle, it follows that an ontological conception of truth also entails the independence principle. This makes sense; after all, according to the ontological conception of truth, the notion of truth is precisely the notion of objective and independent truth, where "independence" here means independent of human thought. Suppose that human beings were to disappear from the face of the earth tomorrow, along with all other life forms in the universe that have a capacity for conscious experience. The metaphysical realist and the ontological truth theorist would both hold that in such a world there would still be objective facts of the matter about the way things are, which is just to say that there would still be truths about various states of affairs in this post-conscious world. From what perspective would there be objective truths in this world, you ask? A God's-eye point of view would fit the bill nicely, assuming there is a God, but failing that, realism requires the existence of some impersonal, external, objective perspective. Antirealists regard the very idea of such a perspective to be absurd, but for the metaphysical realist it is nothing less than the article of faith upon which the intelligibility of the world around us depends.

7.2: SELF-REFERENCE, TRUTH, AND THE KINK IN THE CARPET

We noted in our survey of theories of truth in Chapter Two that a curious problem arises concerning the truth of statements that refer to themselves. The example we considered there was the case of an Australian who says: *All Australians are liars.* An even more general and directly self-referential sentence that does not rely on the identity of anyone who utters it is this: *This sentence is false*, which, if you think about it, seems to be true if it really is false, and false if it really is true. We also considered a way to get around these so-called paradoxes of self-reference in the philosophy of language. If we invoke a hierarchy of languages so that we can defer talk of the truth of a statement in a language to a metalanguage, we have an escape route known as semantic ascent. As it turns out, however, the phenomenon of self-reference is responsible for some of the most exciting discoveries in philosophy of the last century. In this final section, we touch on some of these results and relate them to truth and to metaphysics.

Some beings and systems are capable of referring to themselves, while others are not. You are capable of referring to yourself, of course, and do so whenever you use a first-person pronoun such as "I," but the mug sitting on the desk in front of me is incapable of self-reference. In 1931, Gödel devised an ingenious demonstration of the fact that some formal languages, including arithmetic, are capable of referring to themselves. The shock waves generated by this proof continue to reverberate throughout logic and mathematics, and indeed its impact in those areas invites comparison with, say, the impact Darwin's theory had on biology. I would argue that if one subscribes to an ontological conception of truth, Gödel's result also has important implications for metaphysics.

In the case of mathematics, Gödel's result means that the capacity of systems such as arithmetic to generate truths, or theorems, outstrips the capacity of such systems to prove those truths. Gödel's proof makes use of the same technique of diagonalization that we encountered in Chapter Three as part of a proof of the impossibility of knowing everything there is to know, and in Chapter Five as well, where we noted in passing that Cantor used it to prove the existence of sets of uncountably infinite numbers. For reasons that are very similar to those that led us to semantic ascent as a way of avoiding paradoxes of self-reference in languages, Gödel's result implies that systems capable of expressing self-reference are essentially open-ended with respect to truth. The word logicians use to describe the open-ended nature of truth in Gödelian systems is *incomplete*, but the incompleteness of a system is subject to an important technical qualification: Gödel proved that systems such as arithmetic are incomplete only if they are *consistent*—that is, free of contradictions.

Now if one adopts the position that truth is no mere artifact of language or the mind, but that it is rather essentially metaphysical in nature, then, unless truths with respect to formal systems such as arithmetic are somehow different in kind from other truths, *Gödel's Incompleteness Theorem* (as it is known) has implications for metaphysics as well as for formal systems. If, then, arithmetic truths are simply some truths among others in the world of truths, which does not seem to me to be an unreasonable assumption, then the totality of truths must forever elude our grasp. In other words, if truths generated by self-referential, Gödelian systems are accorded the same ontological status as any other truths, then there is a very real sense in which, as Patrick Grim (1950–) argues, what Gödel has done is to demonstrate that ours is an incomplete universe. What kind of thing is truth, ontologically speaking? Is it mind-like or does it constitute some other kind of ontological category? We do not know, and indeed the answer does not affect my point here. In any case, given my argument that the sum of truths is ultimately elusive, it should not come as a surprise that there may be truths about the nature of truth that elude us. Summing up, to the extent that the ontological conception of truth is correct and that the nature of truth itself is open-ended, then the world itself is open-ended or incomplete—provided that the world does not somehow embody a contradiction. What it might mean for the world itself to embody a contradiction is an important question, further consideration of which is beyond the scope of this book.

Is the universe unified, whole, and composed of one thing alone, or does the universe comprise a Many? If metaphysical realism and the ontological conception of truth hold, then at least one thing—alternatively, at least one truth—exists independently of me. But in this case at least two things exist: I exist and also whatever exists independently of me, which means pluralism prevails and the universe is a Many. On the other hand, if nothing exists independently of me, then we are left with subjectivism, antirealism, and monism. Remember, however, that nothing can make this objectively true, because in this case there is no perspective other than one's own with respect to which it can be true! To the extent that "truth" could mean anything at all in this case, then it would be "truth" for me alone. In fact, the very idea of truth becomes contradictory, a theme common to various mystical traditions and one which helps explain why mystics tend to be very much at home with monism.

If pluralism holds true, does the world consist of many things of a single kind, or of many things of different kinds? Are truth and the world mind-like, or are they ontologically different in kind from mind? We do not know, but all of these possibilities are open, and the answer consists in the very nature of the universe itself.

This brings to a close our brief survey of Western philosophy. As I noted at the very beginning of the book, there are philosophical traditions other than the Western tradition, and other ways of thinking about ourselves and the world. The open-endedness of truth allows for this plurality of worldviews and philosophies. But if truth really is open-ended and if we have anything at all to learn from this, it is that those other traditions, worldviews, and philosophies must concede the possibility that some truth might even have found its way into the pages of this book.

Imagine trying to lay a carpet in an infinite room that stretches out endlessly in all directions. Obviously, the carpet itself would need to be infinite, and you would never be able to complete the task of laying it. Now imagine laying a carpet in an ordinary room, but suppose that the carpet is too big for the floor of the room. If a carpet is too big to fit the room it's in, it forms a bubble, or kink, which persists no matter how hard you try to get rid of it. Your room is complete, as it were, but the flaw in the carpet that comes with it will elude you and reappear somewhere else in the room if you try to stamp it out once and for all. This is roughly analogous with truth in Gödelian systems. The open-ended carpet is flawless but you can never finish the job of laying it, while the complete room has a serious drawback, in that the carpet that accompanies it is fatally flawed, or kinky. We can iron out any specific inconsistency in a Gödelian system by amending the system, but the problem will inevitably reappear somewhere else in the system. What sort of carpet we are dealing with depends on what kind of room we inhabit, where the room is the universe itself. Is the room an endless, inexhaustible, and consistent one, or is it infected with elusive and ineradicable inconsistency? Which kind of room do we live in? No one knows, but due to another theorem Gödel proved, the consistency of a Gödelian system cannot be proved within that system and so we cannot prove that we will never come across a kink in our carpet. It is our duty as philosophers to remain on the lookout for one, however, and I wish you luck in your search.

Further Reading

It is often said in philosophical circles that there is no substitute for reading the original works of great philosophers, or primary sources. This is quite true, but on the other hand there is no need for a beginner to take on the complete works of Hegel or Kant as an entry point to the study of philosophy. Fortunately, most of the classic texts in philosophy are readily available in larger bookstores, libraries, and online. What follows is a short, annotated list of relatively accessible readings that includes primary, secondary, electronic and online resources.

DICTIONARIES AND ENCYCLOPEDIAS

Audi, Robert, ed. *The Cambridge Dictionary of Philosophy*. 2nd ed. Cambridge: Cambridge UP, 1999. Slightly more thorough than *The Oxford Companion to Philosophy*, this is perhaps the best of the single-volume dictionaries of philosophy, although it does not include entries on living philosophers.

Craig, Edward, ed. *Routledge Encyclopedia of Philosophy*. London: Routledge, 1998, Vols 1–10. Also available on CD-ROM, this is a comprehensive and worthy rival to *The Encyclopedia of Philosophy* as an all-purpose reference work.

Edwards, Paul, ed. *The Encyclopedia of Philosophy*. New York: Macmillan and the Free Press, 1967, volumes 1–8, with Supplement, 1996. Long the standard encyclopedia in the field, this somewhat dated work was brought up to date with the addition of a new, supplementary volume in 1996. It remains a reliable place to start for extended articles and biographies on a wide range of topics.

Honderich, Ted, ed. *The Oxford Companion to Philosophy*. Oxford: Oxford UP, 1995. Similar in size and scope to *The Cambridge Dictionary of Philosophy*, this work is slightly less comprehensive than its competitor, but does include entries on living philosophers.

Martin, Robert. *The Philosopher's Dictionary*. 2nd ed. Peterborough, ON: Broadview, 1994. This pocket-sized dictionary is a handy reference for concise definitions and descriptions of philosophical terms and philosophers.

PRIMARY SOURCES

Hume, David. *Dialogues Concerning Natural Religion*. Indianapolis, IN: Hackett, 1980. Largely devoted to a critique of the argument from design for God's existence, Hume's arguments are lively and stimulating, if not always fully persuasive. The Hackett editions of philosophical classics are economical, accessible and widely available.

Kant, Immanuel. *Prolegomena to Any Future Metaphysics*. Indianapolis, IN: Hackett, 1977. The Prolegomena, as it is popularly called, is an excellent introduction to Kant's systematic philosophy. For an introduction to Kantian ethics, see his *Grounding for the Metaphysics of Morals*.

Mill, John Stuart. *Utilitarianism*. Indianapolis, IN: Hackett, 1979. Concise and elegant, Mill's essay remains the standard statement of utilitarianism in its original form.

Plato. *The Last Days of Socrates*. Harmondsworth, Middlesex: Penguin, 1954. This is ostensibly an account of the trial and death of Socrates, in which Plato incorporates some of the important ethical teachings of Socrates in four short dialogues which together make a highly digestible, timeless, and superbly written literary masterpiece. This edition is translated and introduced by Hugh Tredennick.

Russell, Bertrand. *The Problems of Philosophy*. New York: Oxford UP, 1997. Originally written in 1912, this new edition features an introduction by John Perry. An elegant classic, Russell's book is a rare example of philosophy that is at once accessible for beginners and required reading for professionals in the fields of epistemology and metaphysics.

GENERAL

Bailey, Andrew. *First Philosophy: Fundamental Problems and Readings in Philosophy*. Peterborough, ON: Broadview, 2002.

Dancy, Jonathan. *Introduction to Contemporary Philosophy*. Oxford: Blackwell, 1985. Written at the advanced beginner level, this is an excellent, thorough and balanced survey of theories in epistemology.

Govier, Trudy. *God, the Devil and the Perfect Pizza*. Peterborough, ON: Broadview, 1989. Very accessible and ideal for beginners, these dialogues on questions such as free will, determinism, the existence of God and artificial intelligence offer highly digestible food for thought.

Nagel, Thomas. *What Does it all Mean? A Very Short Introduction to Philosophy*. New York: Oxford UP, 1989. Aimed at an upper-level high school readership, Nagel's exposition and ideas about such topics as God, existence and knowledge are a very good starting point for beginners.

Passmore, John. *A Hundred Years of Philosophy*. 2nd ed. London: Penguin, 1966. This is a detailed and informative survey of twentieth-century analytic philosophy.

Perry, John, and Michael Bratman, eds. *Introduction to Philosophy*. 3rd ed. New York: Oxford UP, 1998. One of many standard textbooks for first-year undergraduate philosophy survey courses, Perry and Bratman's offering features a particularly good selection of excerpts and articles, and tends to be a little more advanced than other titles in the field.

Rucker, Rudy. *Infinity and the Mind*. London: Paladin, 1982. Rucker's book goes well beyond the beginner's level, but is a fascinating overview of the philosophy and mathematics of infinity. It is the inspiration of the main argument in § 3.6.

Solomon, Robert C. *Introducing Philosophy*. 6th ed. Forth Worth, TX: Harcourt Brace, 1997. Another very good introductory survey text, this volume of readings and commentaries features material on existentialism, aesthetics, and feminism.

ELECTRONIC AND ONLINE

Kolak, Daniel. *The Philosophy Source*. CD-ROM. Wadsworth. A library of classic texts in convenient CD-ROM form, this covers philosophers from the ancient Greeks to the twentieth-century American pragmatists.

The Internet Encyclopedia of Philosophy. <http://www.utm.edu/research/iep/>. Well organized and comprehensive, this is an excellent online resource.

The Stanford Encyclopedia of Philosophy. <http://plato.stanford.edu/contents.html>. Ed. Edward Zalta. This online encyclopedia is user-friendly and rapidly becoming a standard online source for philosophy.

The World-Wide Web Virtual Library: Philosophy. <http://www.bris.ac.uk/Depts/Philosophy/VL/>. This is a very useful portal to an extensive range of philosophy sources around the Web.

Index

Index

Cicero, 1
cogito ergo sum, 76
cognition, 46, 49–50, 82
coherence theory of truth, 57–58
communication systems, 45
communication theory, 89–90
computation, 40
computer programming, 45
computer science, 54
conceptual schemes, 83
continental philosophy, 8
contingent truths, 66–67
continuous vs. discrete concepts, 139–41
contractarians, 118–19
contradictions, 60
correspondence theory of truth, 57–58, 62, 63
cosmological argument for existence of God, 158–61, 172
cosmology, 144–45
counterfactuals, 39
Cratylus, 21, 136–39
cultural differences, 104–07

Darwin, Charles, 27, 79–81, 82, 119, 161, 167, 185
Dawkins, Richard, 167–68, 174
death, religion and, 171–74
Declaration of Independence, 119
deconstruction, 42
Dedekind, Richard, 140
deductive arguments, 51–52
definite description, 47–48
democracy, 109–10
Democritus, 19
dependent vs. independent beings, 29
Derrida, Jacques, 41, 42
Descartes, René, 7, 25, 28–29, 31, 35, 39, 73–76, 82, 84, 127, 153, 157
description, knowledge by, 88
descriptions, theory of, 47–48
descriptive metaphysics, 38
descriptive theories of ethics, 103
design, arguments from, 160–61
determinacy, identity and, 136–39
determinism vs. free will, 18, 31, 34–36
Dewey, John, 58
diagonalization, 147, 185
dialectic, 36–37
dictionaries, 46
discourse, 42
discrete vs. continuous concepts, 139–41
doctrine of eternal recurrence, 145
dogma, 19, 152
Donnellan, Keith, 48
dual-aspect theory, 30
Dummett, Michael, 56

early modern period, metaphysics in, 28–36
efficient cause, 159

eidos, 23
Einstein, Albert, 130–32, 134–35
Empedocles, 19
empiricism, British, 79, 81, 88
empiricist methodology, 14
Engels, Friedrich, 165
Ephesus, 18
epistemology, 42, 55, 69–97, 129; evolutionary, 80–81
equality, 107–13
esse est percipi, 32
essential properties, 26–27, 136–37
ether, 128
ethical relativism, 104–07
ethics, 8, 26, 98–124; descriptive and prescriptive theories of, 103, 108; Kantian, 113–16; language of, 99–104; utilitarian, 107–13; virtue, 117–18; vs. morals, 104
eudaimonia, 117–18
Evans, Gareth, 48
evil, problem of, 168–70
evolutionary epistemology, 80–81, 83
existence, nature of, 17–42
existentialism, 8, 13, 41, 120

fact-value dichotomy, 101–02
facts, ethics and, 99–104; propositions and, 38–39
faith, reason and, 152–54
feminist theory, 15, 120–23
Fichte, J.G., 36
first-order logic, 55
"Five Ways", 158–61
Fodor, Jerry, 50
form, matter and, 26–27
formal languages, 45, 60–62, 184
Forms, Platonic, 23–26
forms of intuition, 129–30
Foucault, Michel, 41, 42
free will vs. determinism, 18, 34–36
Frege, Gottlob, 47, 54, 62–63
Freud, Sigmund, 41, 166–67, 174
functional organization, 40–41

Gadamer, Hans-Georg, 41
Galilei, Galileo, 35, 131, 146
game theory, 163
Gassendi, Pierre, 31
Gauthier, David, 118
generalizations, inductive, 34, 53
genetics, 105–06, 123
geometry, 20, 28, 83, 139–141
Gettier, Edmund, 86–87
Gilligan, Carol, 121
God, existence of, 36, 59, 82, 128–29, 152–54, 170–75; Anselm on, 155–57; Aquinas on, 158–61; critics of, 165–68, 174–75; evil and, 168–70; Kierkegaard on, 162; Pascal on, 162–64
God or Nature, 31

Index

Index

mind-body interaction, 29–36
Minkowski, Herman, 132
modal logic, 67
monads, 30
monism, 30, 181–82, 186
monotheism, 152–53
Moore, G.E., 37, 78
moral conclusions, 103
morals, 107–20, 121–22; ethics vs., 104

Nagel, Thomas, 177
natural languages, 45
natural law theories, 119–20
necessary falsehoods, 67
necessary truths, 66–67
necessity, possibility and, 159–60
Neumann, John von, 54
neural states, 40
neuroscience, 40
Newton, Isaac, 35, 53, 127–29, 131–32, 141
Nietzsche, Friedrich, 36, 120, 145, 165–66
Noddings, Nel, 121
normative statements, 102
noumenal realm, 82

objective conception of truth, 63–65, 178–80
objectivity, 121; vs. subjectivity, 2, 13, 176–80
objects, 46–47
observation, 19
One-Many problem, 180–84, 186
ontological argument for existence of God, 155–57
ontological conception of truth, 63–65,
    178–80, 185–87
ontological pluralism, 182–83
ontology, 18, 29, 30
open-endedness, 8
ordinary language philosophy, 39
outer experience, 130

Paley, William, 160
paradoxes of induction, 53–54
paradoxes of infinity, 145–46
paradoxes of Zeno, 21–22, 133–34
Parmenides, 20–22, 27, 30, 133–35, 181
Pascal, Blaise, 162–64, 172, 174
Pascal's Wager, 163–64
payoff matrix, 162–63
Peirce, Charles Sanders, 58
phenomenal realm, 82
phenomenology, 41
philosophical psychology, 77
philosophy, ancient Greek, 18–28; competing
    conceptions of, 7–12; contemporary, 36–42;
    definition of, 1–16; early modern, 18–36;
    medieval, 26, 54; the word, 4–7
philosophy-as-wisdom, 4–5
physical vs. non-physical, 29
physics, 9–10, 25–26, 39, 56, 125–49; change
    in, 139–41

pineal gland, 29
Planck's constant, 141
Plato, 5, 8, 13, 22–26, 31, 64, 86, 122, 135,
    152
pleasure, 109
plenum, 127
pluralism, 30, 182–83, 186
political philosophy, 15
Popper, Karl, 174
positivism, logical, 37–38
possibility, necessity, 159–60
possible worlds, 67
postmodernism, 8, 15, 41
powers, 31–32
pragmatic theory of truth, 58–59
pre-established harmony, doctrine of, 30
Pre-Socratics, 7, 19–22, 29, 42, 73, 133
prescriptive statements, 102
prescriptive theories of ethics, 103, 108
primary qualities, 31–32, 79
primordial element, 18–19
principle of bivalence, 55–56
principle of non-contradiction, 55
principle of sufficient reason, 128–29
principle of verifiability, 37–38
process, philosophy of, 37
properties, essential vs. accidental, 26–27,
    136–37
propositions, 38–39, 55, 61, 84
Protagoras, 42
psychoanalysis, 166
psychology, 4, 40, 47, 50; philosophical, 77
Putnam, Hilary, 48, 58, 75, 177
Pythagoras, 20

qualities, primary vs. secondary, 31–32, 79
quantification, 54–55
quantity vs. quality, 27
quantum mechanics, 141
quantum physics, 56, 139, 141
quantum theory, 39
Quine W.V., 5–6, 50, 58, 67

radical skepticism, 78
rational vs. irrational numbers, 20
rationalist methodology, 13–14
rationality, 46, 121
real numbers, 140
realism, metaphysical, 39, 65, 176–80, 183–84
reality, 7, 8, 142; appearance vs., 22–25;
    language and, 38–39; nature of, 17–42
reason, 5, 19, 44–68; faith and, 152–54
reasoning, 51–56
reference, 45–51; causal theory of, 48–49;
    descriptivist theory of, 47–48
Reflection Principle, 148–49
relative motion, 131–32, 159
relative space and time, 127–29, 131–32
relativism, 59–60; ethical, 104–07

Index

relativity, theories of special and general, 130–32
relativity of simultaneity, 131–32
religion, 1, 24; philosophy of, 150–75
reversibility, 113–14
Richard's Paradox, 92
Rorty, Richard, 58
Rucker, Rudy, 92
rule utilitarian ethics, 112
Russell, Bertrand, 8, 12, 37, 47–48, 54, 88
Ryle, Gilbert, 40

Samos, 18
Sapir-Whorf hypothesis, 49
Sartre, Jean-Paul, 41, 120
Saussure, Ferdinand de, 42, 50
Schelling, Friedrich, 36
Schopenhauer, Arthur, 36
science, 2, 4, 9–10, 25–27, 31, 53, 58, 125–49
Scotus, Duns, 28
Searle, John, 48
secondary qualities, 31–32, 79
self-reference, 3, 184–87
semantic theory of truth, 60–62
semantics, 46, 55
semiotics, 15, 41–42, 50
sensations, 31–32
sensory knowledge, 74–76
set theory, 147–48
Sextus Empiricus, 73
Shannon, Claude, 89
ship of Theseus, 138
signs, 45
Singer, Peter, 112
Sinn, 47
skepticism, 36, 72–78, 177; Cartesian, 73–76;
    Humean, 76–78, 81; radical, 78
Skinner, B.F., 40
Smart, J.C.C., 40, 130
social contract, 118–19
social philosophy, 15
Socrates, 4–5, 6, 22, 27, 71
solipsism, 91, 179–80
space, time and, 126–32
space-time, 132
speculative metaphysics, 38
Spinoza, Baruch, 30–31, 127, 134, 181
state of nature, 119
steady state theory of cosmology, 144
Strawson, P.F., 38, 48
structural linguistics, 42
subjectivity vs. objectivity, 2, 13, 176–80, 186
substance, 26, 29–36; attribute vs., 27
superstition, 19
syllogistic logic, 26, 54
syntax, 45, 55
synthesis, 37
synthetic truths, 65–68

Tarski, Alfred, 60–62
teleological argument for existence of God,
    158–61
teleology, 27
Thales, 19
theodicy, 168–70
theology, 28, 152–53
theory of descriptions, 47–48
Theory of Everything, 9–10
thesis and antithesis, 37
Thomism, 28
time, change and, 132–35; passage of, 130;
    space and, 126–32
time dilation, 131
transfinite numbers, 148
translation of languages, 5–6, 49–50
truth, 8, 44–68, 178–80; self-reference and,
    184–87; theories of, 56–65
truths, analytic, synthetic, necessary and
    contingent, 65–68; of mathematics and
    logic, 25
Turing, Alan, 41, 54

Übermensch, 120
unboundedness, 142–43
uncertainty principle, 141
United States Constitution, 119
universal grammar, 50
universality, 6
universalizability principle, 113–16
universes, open vs. closed, 143–45
unknowable, knowable and, 90–97
utilitarian ethics, 107–13
utility principle, 107–09

vacuum, 127
value judgments, 102
values, facts, ethics and, 99–104
verifiability, principle of, 37–38
via negativa, 1
view from nowhere, 177
virtue ethics, 117–18

Watson, J.B., 40
Whitehead, A.N., 5
will to power, 120
Wilson, E.O., 119
wisdom, 4–5, 97; received, 19
wish fulfillment, 166
Wittgenstein, Ludwig, 10, 38–39, 44
Wollstonecraft, Mary, 120
women's rights, 120–21
world-line, 135
worldview, language and, 49, 58

Xenophanes, 150, 174

Zeno, 21–22, 96, 133–34, 140–41

196